The birds, the bees, and the human species

The birds, the bees, and the human species

A Grand Climax

Series: Part one

Written by

Jerr

Illustrations by

Bruno Solís de Campos

Dedicated to fatherless men

Introduction

The start of a book on sex must concern itself with base principles. Theories and hypotheses are only as strong as their root to foundational realities. This book is not a sex manual but rather an introduction into understanding the what sex means to our species. What does sex mean to the female and what does sex mean to the male? The book you are holding will explore the most basic of principles of sexual behavior with men and women in order to build a solid foundation for the thesis.

There is a saying in reference to the "birds and bees" as a means for parents to have the sex talk with their children. The truth of sex is not just something we hold as a human species but rather a grand truth of all living things on earth. A desire for opposite sexes to harmonize and replicate themselves from compulsion to biological imperative. The book will start small and then will expand out in scope once the base foundations of thought have been laid firm in mind. Once the core is understood, the concept can take hold in comprehension.

Some aspects of the book will seem moralistic in my explanations for the existing world and the state of sexual behavior. This does not mean that I view myself as morally superior as much as I view writing as an act of truth seeking regardless of my own personal decision making and life choices. This means that I write to give the best possible advice for men who want to know the truth even if the messenger stumbles and falls. The responsibility

I bear is that I give direction that leads to your success and away from your failure.

We are an imperfect fatherless generation who fear to speak because we feel we have no room to talk. Our tongues freeze up in our mouths only because we feel shame in our behavior. The bravery starts with speech and brave thoughts do not require us to be perfect but require us to be willing to share the truth regardless if it condemns ourselves along with others.

Sexual beginnings

A man's genitalia are outside himself and a woman's genitalia are inside herself. Men hold their sexual organ before their eyes to urinate from a young age. We look upon ourselves and aim our stream of urine out from our member. Just as an arrow from a bow is cast from the hand of a hunter with precision from his eye, the same can be said of a man and his own sexual meaning. We objectify ourselves and environments by not only holding in familiarity our penises but by controlling the flow of our urinations. A young boy will use his stream of urination in play as he focuses and directs the stream on objects. It could be the side of a tree, the side of a toilet bowl or a leaf on the ground.

The male sexual organ is outside the body but within our gaze and exposed to the light of the world. It represents a casting of our will upon the world just as arrow from bow. The casting of an arrow from a boy is a fear of imagination and will. We must point with our body and focus with our mind. To cast aim is to imagine. Before a man pierces the bullseye of a target, he must already see the arrow dead center in his mind's eye. His mind is already there and his body must play catch up. The same with a man and his stream of urination. He stands upright and tall with a view of himself and environment to direct his flow to where he gazes. All psychological meaning is built upon biology necessity. A man's own sexual psychology is conditioned by his own experience with his body. The way a man navigates the world is how he first learned to navigate his body. Men are visually based because our bodies train us to be visually based. We objectify women and the world around us because we first learn to objectify ourselves. The supreme object for a man is his own sexual organ. It is an object of not only necessity but play as the stream of urine is a biological representation of stream of consciousness. The hand that holds the penis becomes like a hand that holds a tool that performs an objective mission of relief. Holding the member, aiming and directing the stream are all experiences withing the **male gaze** therefore solidifying its meaning within the male's sexual psychology.

The most intelligent predators in the animal kingdom are the ones that spend the most time in play. Play is an experimentation of the configurations of self with the configurations of environment. The human male learns to play with his environment from his beginning years with his own stream of urination based on the direction of his mind's eye. "What would it look like wet?" "What would happen if I peed on that?" "How much of a splash would I get if I peed farther or closer to myself?" All these questions go through a young man's mind as he experiments with his own body with the environment that surrounds him. Even a father or mother will teach a young boy about aiming his urine in a more precise way as not to splash on the lid of the toilet or outside the bowl. The play with urine becomes a game with rules of precision and focus. New objectives form as mastery is pursued.

A human female's sexual organ is hidden from her sight. Her member is within her body and minimally outside unlike the male. She does not need to hold, direct and aim her stream of urine. Her main concern is squatting in such a way as to avoid urination upon herself. She must trust her pose with her entire body and not just her hands to allow her to splash below and not upon herself. Her sexual organ and stream of urination is beyond her eye which diffuses the meaning away from a clear objective to one of holistic understanding across her whole body.

A young woman is trained to hold more meaning in her imagination and not the objective reality with her eyes. She must hunch down close to the earth to relieve herself which is a further blinding of her visual gaze upon the world. Close to the earth and urinating from an unseen area of her body, her stream flows out beyond her eye and only can be discerned by subtle intuitions within her mind. This biological training influences her to rely on intuition and playful imaginings of possible meanings. Unlike the clear objective of male urination with its visual play, a female's urination is one of pure necessity devoid of play. The only thought is of avoiding splash on the hams of her body and clothes. She squats down closer to the earth in ritualistic display of oneness with nature as opposed to the male who stands above the earth to gaze upon what he seeks dominion over with his stream.

The inbuilt aspect of biological play informs a male's sexual selection which I will discuss later in this book and the inverse lack of biological play informs a female's sexual selection. The female who must urinate beyond her eye will naturally fetishize the importance of intuition over objective rationalization. Her own genitalia that is unseen from her eye will inform her psychology to view her body as a lightning rod of sensations to pick up on meanings that a male gaze could not understand. She will romanticize emotional intuition over objective rationalization because her body trains her to do so. What cannot be seen or understood with eyes will be viewed as deep female wisdom. Women will innately feel at one with environments and the earth because they view themselves as sages to the climate of reality. The urinating squat of a female is like a prayer to feminine psychology of getting closer to nature by relief of mystery. A male's expression of urination is one in the light of his sight while the female's expression is one in the darkness of her mind. *Objective light and subjective dark.* This must be understood to understand the sexual behaviorism and arousal of our species. We must understand the body that we were gifted with from birth and infancy to understand how the psychology was formed from that frame.

Darkside of the moon

When a man is first learning about female arousal, he will hear that "women fall in love with their ears." This is a fundamental difference between men and women. While a man can become highly aroused by visual pornography, a woman is more aroused by erotic fiction. The reason why women are more aroused by reading than viewing is that a woman becomes aroused by her own imagination. Reading is a practice in imagination. When a woman is reading a book, she will paint with the brush of her imagination the scenes she is exploring. While a writer will describe in detail the story and characters, it is the reader who truly forms the imagery in the mind. Remember, a woman's sexual interest is formed around her biological necessity. A woman's sensitive clitoris is outside her eye which becomes a vague feeling that takes hold in her imagination. While a man's sexual heat is focused within his gaze, a woman's sexual heat is diffused and dispersed across her body from the lack of clear sight. What is out of sight must be understood within mind.

The mystery of a woman's sexual organ places her in the dark of her desire. What happens when we are in the darkness? We must rely on touch, sound and imagination. These three are the core framework of female sexual heat. A woman's confusion over the center of her heat imbues her in whole. This is why blowing on the ear of a female or gently touching her arm or her lower back can build sexual heat. Her sexual heat is blind and must be led by the one with sight. When a man is on a date with a woman, he leads her through the experience and even will lead her by the hand as they walk. She is blind in her passion and he is leading her to the heart of the mystery. The diffused understanding of her heat makes her electrified by the man who is certain in his own desire. His knowing touch melts her like butter on the toast of his sexual want.

A woman cannot direct her own sexual pleasure no more than the blind can lead the blind. It is the certainty of a man's direction which allows a woman to feel safe in her submission. This involves the same amount of trust of someone without sight being led by someone with sight. The hand in the dark that takes another can either fill the heart with relief or terror. A woman's sensitivity brings high fear and high arousal. There are a couples who roleplay with blind folds. But this is the fundamental state of a female arousal. It further places the woman in a passive state of submission where she must be led. All the senses beyond sight are heightened as touch and sound fuel erotic fantasy. Just as a blind fold requires trust so does all female sexuality. A woman wants to submit in sex just as the blind wants to trust those who guide. But trust must be earned which is the reason why a man's masculine frame is the psychological reassurance that women seek.

It is common for woman to describe their sexual fantasies as a feeling rather than an objective experience. A woman can say that she feels a warm uprising that washes over her like summer's tide on the beach. Does that sound sexual to a man? No. But to a woman, a warm blanketed experience describes her sexual heat that is diffused across her body. In the dark room of her mind, it is the surrounding air and the anticipation of a presence that builds the necessary energy of excitement. A woman is waiting in sexual passivity for the hand to reach out at her from the darkness. With eyes closed and electric feel. Breath on neck and a feeling of warmness of a hand yet to touch skin. It is the frozen anticipation of a mystery to be revealed that casts the deepest spell on a woman's mind. What is about to happen and the possibilities that surround. Million shattered pieces of sexual intent that spin around the erotic fantasy. The waiting for the man to make a move and the mystery of where he will lead is the heat-of-wait that bears down on the woman's body. It is an undescribed passion that can only be articulated as a *feeling*. This is the same of a blind man describing a sunset or sunrise. Place him in the ray of light of a sunset and he will describe the fading absence of warmth on his skin. Place him in the twilight of a rising sun and he will describe the cold being taken away and replaced with the warm embrace of sunshine. A man may be able to see the sunrise but only a woman truly understands what it means to be embraced by its warmth.

Sight and hunger

A man's sexual arousal is focused on his sight. It is the revelation of a woman's body that most excites him. The male gaze objectifies a woman's body as an instrument of pleasure. Men will excite themselves over specific body parts on a woman's body. It could be a woman's ass, her breasts or her legs. Each part of a woman is fetishized in passion. A man looks upon a woman as something to be consumed like a hungry man feasting at a banquet. But just as important as the dish before a man is the light that allows him to know what he is eating. We can get excitement about satisfying our hunger when we eat by the mere anticipation of the appearance of the food. The mouth will water from the sight of food as the anticipation runs over like water from a glass. This is the same with sex for a man. It is the female's form that most entices a man in his own heat. It is the object of his eye that he focuses his pleasure towards and the anticipation of his hand transcending the space between to the object of his desire. This is the same as the mouth waters from looking upon food, to holding it in hand, to being eaten. This is the conditioned programming of objectification of penis in sight and hand from youth.

A man can see not only what arouses him from afar but he can also see his own aroused member. It is the eye that most inflames a man into heat. But the imagination is also important to a man even if it is less a necessity as it is to a female. Arousal builds from anticipation of desire yet fulfilled for a man just as it is for a woman.

Men will fantasize about the unseen forms of a woman's beauty. The curve of her body and the shadow of cleavage between her breasts. Imagination of unpeeling a woman's clothes off like a wrapper off a candy. Sugar sweet radiance revealed. The core of a man's sexual heat is based on his gaze paired with the heavy anticipation of touching what he sees. This is the mating ritual of our human species. A woman presents herself in showcase of her body to entice a man's desire for eventual touch. The eye holds the most power in the kingdom of men. It is the eye that holds a woman before the hand does. The male gaze is the penetrative hope for physical release.

The object of man's eye is captured with the object of his own member. But unlike a woman's diffused erogenous zone that covers her entire body, a man's sole erogenous zone is his genitalia. All the energy and blood rushes to a single source between his legs. Hyper focus on a single task as opposed the innate multitasking of a woman's pleasure. Concentration on singular purpose of penetration and propagation. Just as the eye itself unfocused can bring into itself a widened peripheral vision, a female is wide open in her own arousal as opposed to the man's narrowed focus on singular objective. First a man owns a woman by sight before he possesses her by hand. This is a dual process of our own sexual heat which women are well aware of and why women feel violated not just by a man's touch but also by his eyes. They understand that the eye is the beginning of male heat and that inflamed eyes fuel unwanted advances.

The reason why a man becomes aroused by a woman's body is that he wants to possess it with his own. As the penetrator in sexual selection of our species, a man must transcend the boundaries of clothes and flesh to enter the realm of a female's wet acceptance. First a female must catch a man's eye in sexual display before approach, initiation of touch and sexual release. It is the lessened necessity of imagination in the bare reality of form that shapes a man's thoughts towards desire. The female body in the reflected eye of a man is the beginnings of sexual want. The curves and shape of the eye become one with the object before it. The male gaze is equally important in sexual selection as a woman's imagination. A man examines in fine detail what he desires from a distance because he craves to know more in closer inspection. Male sexuality starts at sight and builds as the distance is closed between sight and touch.

In darkness

Truth is a battle between light and darkness. When we exist in the dark about something, we are ignorant of its true design. We conjure our own meaning with narrative creation to stabilize ourselves. A generation of men who were taught Darwinism with its eternal conflict of organism in a battle of the fittest were encouraged to surrender their ancient belief systems for one of cold combat. But the one aspect of conflict that men refuse to admit or understand is the conflict of interest between the sexes. That a female will have a separate interest from the male she is sexually interested with. The reason why some men refuse to believe that women have ulterior motives in sexual selection is that these men project the love of their mothers on the women they are attracted to. They will confuse the unconditional love of a mother to child with the conditional love of a romantic partner.

Romantic love is one with a burden of performance where attachment holds conditions to meet. Only once the conditions of romance are met can a female surrender herself to emotional attachment.

When we want the element of surprise and the benefit of the doubt, we must keep someone in the dark of our true intent. This is true of business, war and romance. A man who is reading this who wants to believe in an unconditional romantic love is a fool. What this type of man must realize is that conflict is not a bad thing. We must challenge ourselves to improve and grow in this world and the human species benefits from the conflict between the sexes. Why would a female want to keep a man in the dark about her own sexual motivations and truth of sexual desire? Let us breakdown the sexual selection of our species from the root and climb up the tree of biological meaning. Humans are born to reproduce before death. This is the fundamental truth of human existence and why we are currently alive at this moment. A male is meant to penetrate a female with his semen and the female is meant to bear the child of a male. This is the eternal truth that no one can escape from regardless if they bear children or not. It is a truth that transcends us which means we must humble ourselves to its root. With this in mind, all human behaviorism is based on sexual selection. All human motives have sexual meaning regardless if they are having sex.

The eternal battle of the sexes is one of power of who has the true authority to lead our species. This question first appeared in the garden of Eden when Eve herself usurped God's authority and Adam followed along in obedience to Eve's will. From the beginning, women have wanted power over men just as men want power over women. This was true a thousand years ago and it is true in our times, and it will be true in a thousand years from our times. It is common for families to be divided between the will of the father and the will of the mother. This battle of will is the internal conflict between the sexes that exists eternal. A male and female are like two iron swords that sharpen each other through challenge.

Why would a female want a man to be in the dark about her own sexual motivations? A man needs to think about "feminine mystique" as a mating ritual game that women play. They win the game either way but it allows them to shift their strategy dependent on whether the man fails or succeeds in that game. The woman presents a half-truth and sees what side the man chooses. For example, a woman will say "I want a man who is romantic, who buys me flowers and who makes love," this advice is for the majority of males. A man must remember that females want to reproduce with the strongest seed among men. This is a major reason why women fall into sexual heat around powerful men who lead others. They want to reproduce with a few select men at the top of the power hierarchy because it means they are passing on a strong genetic legacy that will be preserved further into human survival. This means that a woman wants to breed with a few and does not want to breed with most. So, *when a female gives advice to men as a whole, she is giving advice to the men who she does not want to breed with.* The surrounding horde of unattractive males must be pacified with illusions. But remember, a female sets up a game where she wins regardless. If an unattractive male plays by her rules, she will have power over him for her own advantage of resource. And if an attractive male ignores her rules and plays by his own rules, he most sexual arouses her into joining him. This is what a man must realize. It is because a woman wants two things in sexual selection and she will give the advice that is most helpful for her with the majority of unattractive males. She innately knows that a truly arousing male will not follow her advice and if an unattractive male does follow her advice, at least she has secure power over him by him playing her game. The game itself is rigged in her favor. If a man supplicates himself to her, she wins and if a strong enough man provides a game for her to play, she wins.

Females in sexual selection will give "nice guy" advice because they are speaking to the disgusting mob of males that surround them. Of course, they would want that disgusting horde of men who leer at them with the male gaze to play nice and supplicate themselves to them. The core element of a female's sexual selection is based on subterfuge. This is where we get the "feminine mystique" term from and why men will commonly hear that "women are complicated and men are simple." Females secure themselves in sexual selection by the authority they gain through confusing their mate choices. A female convinces a male that she can never be truly understood because the complexity of her nature creates confusion over her desires and motivations. One of the most important strategies in business and war is to understand the opposing force. When the other side of the battlefield cannot be predicted, it causes ineffectual combat. The element of surprise is one of the strongest elements to war, business and romance. A woman is the darkness of mystery and her greatest strength is mystifying men into submission. But also, it is her greatest weakness as the mystery of a man's masculine frame makes her give up the authority that she so readily defends.

When a woman places a man in the dark and keeps him ignorant of her intent, it shifts power to her favor. But there is a deep innate wisdom to a woman's game of subterfuge. Females inherently know that most men should not propagate and should be used in service to the select breeders of the species. When a woman leads the majority of men astray with her advice, it is a way to prevent the majority of men from reproductive access. The men who prove their merit by shattering the frame of female authority are the ones who earned the access of reproduction. They cut through the lies and deceptions in a female's sexual strategy which is the greatest reassurance to a woman's own reproductive anxiety. Why? A woman craves a leader in sexual selection and the way a man proves that he is a leader is by following his own path and not the path of others. This is why a man should not blame women for leading him astray. It is all part of the grand design of our species and makes us stronger. Men must remember that a female takes a giant risk by letting a male impregnate her. And her entire sexual strategy is in not only protecting that mating decision but in preserving the next generation of our human race.

Body of shadow

The heightened experience of a woman in the moment and the innately confusion over her sexuality makes her seek a man who is certain over himself and the world that surrounds him. Think about it like this. A woman is innately in anxiety about her body and from that foundation of anxiety over that confusion she views reality through that lens. Remember, all psychology is built atop biology. How a woman perceives reality is how she *forced to perceive herself*. She exists in the darkness of herself which causes a high anxiety as well as high arousal. This must be understood to understand why women seek calm and decisive leaders in sexual selection. She seeks a man with low anxiety to calm her high anxiety. She sits in the dark and waits to be guided. And what if the man is nervous? What happens when someone who is sitting in the dark feels a touching hand that is shaking from nerves? Does not that make the blind person who is touched even more anxious? This is what a man must realize. A woman is an amplifier of his subtle emotions. She sits in the dark with high intuition about her surrounding space. Women are innately wise to human behaviorism even while not being able to articulate their wisdom.

A woman's greatest wisdom springs from her unconscious mind. It is all a feeling and not a critical thought. What happens to fish that struggles in the water? Its watery splash echoes to predators who prey on weakness. This happens in the water and this happens in the air with bats who rely on sonar. Those who struggle attract those who seek weak game. A nervous man is a like a fish struggling in the water who attracts sharks. Just as a lion looks for the weakest of the herd, human predators look to the weakest of our species to exploit. When a man has nervous issues, what he is signaling is his doubt over his own reality. He is in fear and his body shakes to signal that fear. When a man has anxious behaviorism, he is projecting that anxiety on others. But even more so on a female. Remember, she is in the dark which means that a shaking hand trying to guide her will spike her imagination. The shaking hand is a rattle of death. A female must take tremendous risk to trust a male enough to let him impregnate her. And why in the hell would she want to carry the seed of fear? All things have sexual meaning.

Women seek confident men with leadership skills in romance because women are seeking men to lead them through the sex act. It is that simple. When a man is leading a woman on a date, he is signaling to her that he can lead her through sex. A female has high sex anxiety from her own passivity in sexual selection. Submission is the most vulnerable state to exist in and all females must submit in sex to the penetrator of our species. This is why dating and courting are trials of confident leadership for males. There must be high reassurance for a female to allow a man to lead the sex act. The hand that reaches out from the dark must be steady and certain. The reason a female has high sex anxiety is that we hold anxiety about things we cannot see. Her genitalia are out of sight and so it brings an uncertain anxiety about its nature and pleasure. But all anxiety can easily be turned into pleasure because anxiety itself is a form of excitement. Females are skittish in sexual selection from fear but also this means they can experience tremendous pleasure from the excitement. It is a common manipulation tactic to place a target in an environment where they are a "fish out of water," and must depend on the person leading them. But this truth of a woman's sexuality. She is confused about her sex and if a man knows where he is going will be a further excitement to her as she is led through the chaos of herself.

Imagine a voice in the dark that shakes and trembles speaking to a woman. The woman feels nervous. She waits but there is only silence so she asks the nervous voice questions. If he will not lead, she will feel that she must. "But he is not the one in the dark," she thinks to herself in resentment. Then out of nowhere the nervous voice keeps talking and will not shut up. She can tell that even silence makes him nervous! She is forced to listen to the man talk, talk and talk. He is like a small boy with his mother. He is seeking validation. "How will he be able to lead me if he cannot lead his own self?" she thinks to herself. She can only imagine what his nervous touch would feel like. It makes her shiver. Then after a while of the man dominating the air around her with his speech, a hand reaches out from the dark. It is cold and clammy. She can feel his nervous shake on her skin and feel his clammy sweat on her skin. She innately feels the death signal in the dark as predators sniff at the air that surrounds them. His nervous energy amplifies within her and now she is a nervous wreck. If he cannot navigate the light of his world then how can he navigate her from the darkness?

Next imagine a voice in the dark speaking to a woman, she is nervous and so tests his authority. He passes the tests and she likes his confidence. He makes her feel safe with his calm demeaner. Then after a time of talking, he reaches out to touch her. His touch is soft and certain. She can tell that he is confident in his own view of reality and that he holds low anxiety over sex. This makes her feel safe in her submission. She amplifies his confidence within herself. She vibrates in anticipation of what his sexual plans are for her. All she has to do is follow his direction through the dark. His leadership makes her calm. She can see herself surrendering herself to him. Most importantly, he makes her feel safe and secure.

"But Jerr," a voice calls out from off the page, "Women want danger, not safety…"

Wrong. They want both. A woman wants to *feel safe in danger*. This is where the man comes into play. He acts as protector to the surrounding chaos. This is why action dates work well because the man leads a woman through danger while reassuring her need for safety. This is the same with a man who knows a native language leading a woman through an unknown land. He is the protector and guide through the possibilities of danger. But also, many asshole guys confuse their women by playing both roles of hero and villain. They will get a woman to get emotionally attached, push her away with antisocial behavior and then act as protector to the very behavior that causes their women fear. This is like the mafia offering a business protection from itself. I am not suggesting a man use this tactic but let's be clear on its meaning.

The key thing for a man to realize is that a woman is passive in the darkness of her sexuality. The darkness of her ignorance means she is looking for a sure guide to lead her through her confusion. And since she is in the darkness, she will be hyper sensitive to all anxiety since it triggers worst case scenarios in her imagination.

Passivity and inflated egos

The innate uncertainty a woman carries about her sense of self and sexuality creates a dark void of confusion in her psychology. When something is nothing it also simultaneously becomes everything. Without clear objective borders to frame a thought it becomes all things to fill the imagination. This innate uncertainty over the sex organ and her hormone flux creates a whirlpool of indecisiveness that keeps in her option paralysis. Why are women passive in sexual selection? The biological reason is that they are voids waiting to be filled. But why are they not voids waiting to engulf the objects of their desire? It is the psychological confusion they carry which makes them frozen in sexual decision.

The male has a clear focus on his sexual member which creates a focused psychology on objective meaning. He is the penetrator who must bring decisive meaning to passive confusion of the female. But this also takes us to why a female has a bluffed and inflated sense of self to cover the innate weakness. The one who must wait in passivity for salvation only has the narrative to control. Men cannot complain about a world that is waiting to crush them because they must overcome that world for sexual success. On the other hand, a female does not need to overcome the world for sexual access but merely needs to present herself to it. Being versus becoming. If the world rejects her then it is the world's loss. She is "complete and perfect." She does not need to change for the world, the world needs to change itself to accept her. This is supreme arrogance in sexual selection from the lack of humility needed for adaptation. Women do want to adapt to a world that rejects them, they will shame and gaslight the world into forming itself around their own weakness. Man starts at the bottom of sexual selection and must conform himself to the rules of a female's expectations of his burden of performance. This is why an overweight man who lives with momma will have a challenge in sexual access while an overweight female who lives with momma will still be able to secure sexual access. A man must admit that he is a failure in sexual selection and humble himself by adapting to a system of rules that goes beyond his own existence.

Sexual selection for a man is like climbing up a mountain whereas sexual selection for a woman is like sliding down a mountain. One is more challenging than the other and one is more passive than the other.

But the core reason a woman can be passive and arrogant in sexual selection is that she is more willing to wait. This comes from her being an egg carrying nester. Many females can go into a sexual hibernation while they wait for a high value man. Most men are sexually thirsty which means they are more willing to lose in sexual negotiations which further gives power to women. This is why a woman can put a steep burden of performance on a man but shrug any burden of performance a man may try to place on her. The passivity of a female in sexual selection comes from a place of privilege. She expects the man to sell himself to her because she knows that she does not need to hustle for sexual access. A female merely needs to go out in public and men will approach her. She will reject a series of male attempts that do not meet her high requirements. The female's body is her instrument to attract the male gaze and if she can get the eyes of a high value man to notice her, it will inflate her ego enough to pass over common men who try for her attention.

The ego is all

The ease and privilege of a female in our sexual selection makes her ego inflated beyond that of an average male. She does not need to humble herself in adaptation like a male and therefore has a natural confidence. Most men are either viewed as invisible or repulsive to most women. They believe themselves to be better than these males and therefore will hold tremendously inflated egos. But what a man must realize is that the inflated ego of a female is similar to the ego of a narcissist. A swing of overcompensation of the slave who becomes master. The inflation comes from lack of testing and covers over the true hidden weak sense of self that females innately hold. This is why men who "neg" or tease women will increase their arousal and interest.

A woman holds high amount of confusion over her identity and has natural low self-esteem over her body. The reason why she has a weak sense of self is that lack of clear objectification of her genitalia confuses her from a young age as well as the irrational emotional feeling of her hormone flux during puberty. Added to this is the monthly "curse of menstruation" which brings body horror to a woman when she is first coming into her womanhood. The unknown mystery of her sex calls out from the void with a bloody scream. This transition from her androgenous youth to the shaping of her body brings deep insecurity over her form. This is a one reason why females have more body dysmorphia than males. But there is an additional reason. A female's weak sense of self incites her to external validation which makes her weak to the criticism of others. Women will spend a good portion of their time examining their form in the mirror from the innate confusion they have over their hidden sex but also because they are *trying to see what the male gaze sees.*

When a female's body begins to form into womanly shape, she will begin to get extra positive attention from men which is an emotional reassurance to her need for validation. Remember, internal confusion requires external stabilization. This conditions her to be sensitive to criticism and judgment over the key to that positive attention.

All this must be understood to understand the sexual heat women get from men who can navigate their egos. How a man treats a woman's inflated ego on a date and in the bedroom is how a man builds the sexual heat within her. A man can come out from the invisible blur through provocation to a woman's sense of self. And this triggers the heart of a woman's pulsating pleasure. *Indignation*. Or "how dare you sir." Women crave sexual domination and for a man to be dominate he must want to be on top. This means he must place his authority over a female and think more of himself than the female innately thinks about herself. Women view themselves as queens in sexual selection from their inherent privilege and only become humble when a man tips the invisible crown from their heads. Once a man realizes that a female has an underserved ego that easily crumbles to reveal the weak sense of self that it covers, he will understand the truth of a woman's sexual pleasure.

Reaching

in

the

dark

A woman's mind is one of daydream and imagination. But not of new dreams but of past experiences. The mind of a man is one of planned futures whereas a woman's mind is one of past introductions. When a woman is with a man, she will be comparing him to not only all men that surround him but also all men in her past. She will compare him to her father, her brothers and her past sexual relationships. This is a reason why men should choose females with less past sexual experiences. It is because a female cannot control the past touch comparisons during sex. She will never admit this but women know this is true. They cannot help compare a man's cock size or duration or confidence in sex. And when a woman is unaroused by a man during sex, she will naturally fall into dream. While the man is heavy in sexual heat, the woman is lost in the dark of herself and is thinking about times where she too had the same animal heat. This is why it is common for most females to fantasize about others during the sex act. The man is singularly focused on the female before him because she is the object that he is building his heat upon but the woman in her passivity falls into fantasy because the moment is not capturing her interest.

A woman thinks of the past only because she is not stimulated by the moment. This is the key thing to think about during the sex act. Men must shock their women awake from dream and make the moment overwhelm their minds. The female body is a conduit for sexual pleasure and lightning rod to touch. Sex should ground both parties into the moment and make them *present*.

The problem with many guys is that they try to make sex special with romance and love making to ground the passions but forget to anchor sex to what is base. Remember man is both higher and lower. We hold both heaven and earth within us. We strive above our animal nature but we must never ignore it's power. It is the animal that is the root, ground and base of sexual desire. We can either bring civilization into the bedroom or we can free ourselves of the sex anxiety that it brings. A man who wants to destroy his woman's fantasy is a man who must provoke her awake. This is what is means to truly take possession of another. They are hypnotized by our presence and our presence overwhelms them. Shock and awe. It is like a glowing hand reaching into the darkness to seize us into its grip. A hand that reaches not only around us but also through our body and mind. Total possession. The word I am about to use will offend emotional men but this is the key word to electrifying a woman into the moment. The word is *violate*. But let us define the word first to understand how important it is for the sex act. It means to "break or fail to comply with" or "treat (something sacred) with irreverence or disrespect" But listen closely, rape is wrong. Rape is tyranny and demonic. To violate a female in sex means to break the rules of a civilized behaviorism. It means to be not afraid to be dirty in sex and to not be afraid to make a woman feel dirty. It means to cause indignation or "how dare you" feelings within her body. This arouses her from the provocation against her boundaries. For a female the act of submission itself is a complicated form of indignation. Women hate submitting to the authority of men but they innately understand that only through sexual submission can they achieve their highest pleasure. And this is why most women will agree to like being spanked as foreplay. Why would they enjoy being spanked? Is it because the body of a woman is a lightning rod of erotic passions and all her body is one single erogenous zone? Yes, but that is only a part of the reason. The core reason women like to be spanked is that is playful violation of their dignity and creates a heat from the indignation. This is why a man who playfully teases a woman's dignity will provoke her into sexual heat. She is aroused by the "how dare you" acts that are committed against her sense of dignity. It could be spanking or having her suck on a finger. Sex becomes intimate the more it cannot be performed in public. A woman allows herself to be playfully teased in the bedroom exactly because it is a safe exploration of body violation. And the penetrative act itself is one of violating the woman's body and boundaries with our own. This is why a man should not let his soft emotional nature make him feel that making a woman feel dirty is a bad thing. It grounds her in the moment and captures her attention from one of drifting fantasy. It is the anchor to the present and brings her into the sexual moment.

The reason a lot of men do not like being dirty in sex and feel that they must "make love" to woman is because respecting a female is essential for their own emotional wellbeing. Why? It is because they do not want to see their authority acting undignified or enjoying base desire. It comes from a fear of being the dominant over the female and of not wanting to see females as enjoying animal pleasures. These types of men lift up women as holy angels in reverence and to defile what is holy makes them feel lost in a hell state. But what they do not realize is that they are denying women their own innate pleasure and are being condescending to their passions. Think about how much pressure these men place on a woman by expecting her to not only represent some perfect holy ideal outside the bedroom but also within. Their women's sexuality will be shut down from overwhelming exceptions of purity and will hide themselves away in fantasy. This is why nice guys who "make love" are first cucked by their females' imaginations during the sex act before these females seek out the real thing to satisfy them.

It is a man's job to bring a woman down to earth during sex and to make her think of him. It is the man's job to free a woman of her sex anxiety and to show her that there is nothing wrong with playing in the dirt.

Being free in the dark

Love means to lose sense of self. It means to bring in another person's identity into our own. The act of love is the act of letting go. This is the same for the sex act for men and women. While the male must "let go" like an archer who must not be overly controlling with his arrow, the female must let go completely of herself to fall into sexual pleasure. She must be willing to fall in her submission like falling into arms of another. It is one built on trust. A female must trust a man's sense of self enough to let go of her own sense of self. This is what the act of submission means to woman during sex. She must feel safe to let go in order for her to achieve pleasure. When a woman is guarded and refuses to let go of power dynamics, she is preventing herself from falling into not only love but also heightened arousal.

The core of sexual dysfunction for a female and a male comes from sex anxiety. Both are different. We will first discuss the female's sex anxiety. The first aspect of her anxiety is the fear of losing control. This is based on her own deep reproductive fear. Remember, a female must submit herself to penetration from a male to become pregnant with his seed and to bear his child. What this means is that she must deem this man worthy of her complete body transformation of her flesh as it balloons and expands. This deep fear calls out from the darkness of a female's subconscious mind. A body horror that first whispered sex anxiety with its blood-soaked mystery at the beginnings of her womanhood. The calling of animal change in her womb that would force her to biological possession. This is the fear that echoes loud in a woman innately that makes her hold tightly to the reins of control in the sex act. Women must let go of the barriers that keep them from this primitive mystery in order to allow themselves to be penetrated. It is a system of control upon control that makes them safeguard their sex. But also, it is the surrendering of control that brings them the sexual heat and wet acceptance needed for mating. The female with her weak sense of self is designed for submission to the strong sense of self in the male. The remaining fragments of her identity are clung onto during sexual selection until she forms emotional attachment to the male. This is when a female will align her identity with the male by copying his tastes and philosophies. A man will notice this when the woman he is dating will like the same food he likes, like the same music he likes and will begin a slow imitation into his desires. It is all by design in our species and brings harmony to our sex.

Women desire calm and confident men in sexual selection because the calmness and confidence are the opposite to their innate anxiety. The display of calm composure and certainty of will that most excites a female on a date is a precursor display of the male's low sex anxiety. A woman craves a man to lead her through sex without anxiety. She craves to be with a man who makes it easy for her to "let her guard down." This is because her guard must be down for her to become wet in heat for his penetration. The wet excretion from a female's vagina is the lubrication for reproductive access. Access that must be biological deserving in the preservation in our species. But there is another reason that a female will have sex anxiety. This comes from a female trusting her authority more than she trusts men's authority. When women become idealogues to their own feminist mission of female supremacy, they are abandoning their own pleasure.

Men will notice that dominant females in social interactions will try to drag that same power dynamic into the sex act as they attempt to lead the male through sex. These types of women will celebrate "being on top" and will encourage males to perform oral sex on them in submissive supplication. But what these women refuse to admit is that they are afraid of losing a control and power during sex because of social conditioning from female empowerment. It increases their fear of loss of control which makes their sex even more guarded than other women. Instead of surrendering themselves to animal passion they try to civilize the act with their ideology. A major reason that feminists will have "dead bedrooms" and why feminist men eventually become cucked by their women. Their sex acts are highly guarded of a female's sense of control and power. The same control and power that acts as barrier to their reproductive necessity. Just as clothes must be shed in sex, so must psychological anxieties.

When a female clings to her authority and sense of self in romance and sex, she is holding tightly to dysfunction. A major reason why a female would want to be dominant and controlling in sex is that she overly identifies with the masculine identity. She wants to lead, guide and direct the experience because she has become sexually confused in imitation of the penetrator. The majority of sexual dysfunction comes from sexual confusion. When males become passive and females become dominant, both will experience lessened sexual pleasures. The problem with dominant women is that they only become "strong and independent" because men have failed them in their lives. Whether it was a weak/absent father figure or weak romantic partners, this is what hardens a woman from the fact that she must learn to lead herself from the failure of male leadership in her life. The more that men fail in their leadership roles, the more women will be forced into them. This will cause massive sexual issues as a woman who has learned to be independent of men will find it incredibly challenging to access her own sexual pleasure which is based on the trust of dependence.

The act of submission requires high trust in in letting go of control and power. Women, even many feminists will admit that the path to their own pleasure requires sexual submission. A reason why hardcore feminists will indulge themselves with their weak men in showy roleplay of BDSM. Instead of submitting themselves to the primitive animal passions that creates aroused sex, they bring more civilization into the bedroom with elaborate kink rituals. The bedroom no longer becomes a cage with two naked animals in mating heat but rather a stage play, with more costumes and toys. The act of showy roleplay allows the female to disconnect from the simplicity of her innate design of submissive pleasure. This act of high civilization allows the animal to be denied. And the animal is denied because it exists as only a reminder of the truth of the sexes. Male as dominant leader and female as submissive follower. Of course, feminists will cloak this in mystification with costumed kink as a way of intellectual denial. They refuse to admit the base that exists inherently to their design so that they can build anything they want on top of it. It is a physical representation of sex anxiety that allows preservation of ego based on ideological control. A lot of different roleplays are a hesitant step towards our true intent but masked. When a man becomes brave enough to get what he truly desires in sex, the masks that cover his anxieties will no longer be needed. When a man plays out his dominant fantasies as the penetrator, the woman can fall into the submission necessary for her guards to dissolve away. Each breaking down of barrier and wall built from reproductive anxiety gives way to the heart of her deepest pleasure. The remaining fragments of self are surrendered for the true void of female consciousness as the darkness becomes complete. And then she can not only embrace the light of a man's sense of self established by his authority in the act but also embrace his physical member into herself. Two become one. One flesh. A losing of self for a moment but a gaining of pleasure from that absence.

A woman's sexual pleasure comes through her ability to lose control over self. It is a woman's fear of loss of control that keeps her from sexual pleasure. This hesitance is what protects a woman's womb from undeserving seed as well our entire species from a further burden. A woman must feel safe to let go and trust the man who will provoke her into a new way of feeling. This is all based on a high sex anxiety that women have. It is a core design because of reproductive anxiety. But also, anxiety over confusion of self. A man must show calm during sex to ease the innate anxiety which allows a female to feel safe in letting go which is the foundation of female pleasure.

Sex is a negotiation

The only unconditional love on earth is a mother and her child. A woman will forsake all conditions because her child is an extension of her own self. When a man confused the love of a mother with the love of his own girlfriend or wife is a man who is confused. These types of men are in a mother/son dynamic with their women and will view it as an offense against the idea of "true love" to think about their romantic relationship as a series of negotiations. But what these men do not realize is that a female never surrenders her expectations of a man's burden of performance. These men will allow their females to get fat, not clean the home, deny them sex and have a disrespectful attitude because they think being self-sacrificing is somehow moral in romantic relations. What they do not understand is that they are on the losing side of a negotiation. They think it "high minded" to forsake their own negotiation while letting the female win their negotiations.

There is a steep burden of performance on a male in sexual selection and that same burden is expected to be maintained in a relationship. If a man loses his job, loses his mind or mojo, he will be abandoned by his woman. Does that sound like unconditional love? Of course not. Romantic love is one of conditions and expectations. Sex itself is a series of negotiations. How many men want something specific in sex or just want to have more sex but feel that they are in a begging situation with their women? These men approach their women and ask them for sexual favors. These men try to initiate sex but are rejected. Does that sound like unconditional love?

If the females in their relationships truly were unconditional in love, they would rarely if ever sexual reject their men. They would give their men what they want because they love them and want them to be satisfied. But what we see in most relationships is that a woman becomes accustomed to rejecting her man in sex. Either she controls the time they have sex or she controls what positions they perform. She is the one in power and the man is the one left in want over his desires. The sooner a man realizes that life and love is a series of negotiations, the sooner he can sharpen his power of negotiation to get what he wants from both. What a man must realize is that a framed man in a relationship is never sexually rejected. If a woman is tired or on her period, she will still want to suck a man's cock to satisfy him. Only in rare situations where the woman is sick with flu or other circumstance is sex postponed. It should not be considered normal for a woman to sexually reject a man in a relationship. She will lose respect for the man who she can easily deny sex. Remember, a man's burden of performance must always be maintained and this is why he must place a burden of performance on the female as well. If a man is healthy, he should be craving frequent sex to satisfy his passions.

"But Jerr" a voice calls out "I asked my woman if we could have sex tonight, she said maybe, and then she said she was too tired when I asked her again"

Men who try to bargain with women about sex will lose negotiations. The worst way to approach sex is with verbal asks. This allows the woman easy rejection based on her whims and energy levels. But what a man must realize is that the act of asking itself is viewed as weak to females which makes them lose arousal for sex. Remember, a woman wants a man to be brave, bold and assertive. This is the symbolic elements of the cock that must penetrate her boundaries. When a man assumes silent consent by initiating his sexual desires will allow the female to be free of the responsibility for the act in passive surrender. Think about it like this. When a man verbally negotiates with a female about their sexual behavior in a relationship, it places authority and responsibility upon her for their sex life. He pushes the authority upon her by allowing her the opportunity to decides both their sex lives. But when a man does not verbalize his sexual behavior but merely initiates his desire allows a woman to surrender without argument. Let us go into the mind of a female and listen to her own thoughts. Follow along and behold.

Jim: "Hey sugar pie, want to have sex tonight?"

The woman named Susan thinks "Why is he asking me and not just taking charge? This is weak behavior. I am getting turned off. I wish I could just be swept off my feet by a man who is bold and not afraid of his own desires"

Susan: "It's been a long day; I have a lot of housework to do and I have a migraine"

Jim: "Okay, what if I help you with dishes?"

Susan thinks "He is so desperate for sex and now he wants to simp for it? Him washing dishes is such a turn off. I am even more turned off than before. I wish I could have sex with Roy next door. He would just take what he wanted and not ask"

Susan: "That would be great! And if you want to help with folding clothes would be a big help as well." Susan thinks she is a like a mom with her son who is eager to please her.

Now let us observe Rick and his woman Betty.

Rick comes home from work and slides up behind Betty who is doing dishes. He starts groping her under her clothes. Betty thinks to herself "I am not in the mood but… his touch does feel good. And it would be a nice break from housework. Also, it would cure my migraine I am having. I do not want to reject him and say no. It is just easier to go along with it. And sex is fun…" Rick and Betty have sex.

See the difference? Too many guys are hesitant towards their sexual desires and their women become emboldened against them. The more a man tries to negotiate sex with words with his woman, the more his woman will use words to negotiate sexual rejection. Sexual chemistry is about touch and silent consent. If silent consent cannot be assumed then there is not a romantic relationship in the first place. We do not assume silent consent with strangers, this is why it is a showcase of intimacy between two people. When a woman allows a man to touch and initiate sex, she holds respect for him and is aroused by him. If a man initiates sexual touch with a female and she stops him to say "Aren't you going to ask for consent?" it a signal that he should find another woman to pursue. Verbal consent kills romantic passions. It is only necessary in an autistic generation who do not understand natural chemistry and who have severe sexual baggage from abuse. But even if a female wants verbal consent because she has a history of trauma, she makes herself someone a man should not invest himself with in the beginning stages of a relationship. Remember, it is not a man's role to sacrifice his sexual desires for a woman's benefit. We must carry our high burden of performance and feel no guilt when we expect a woman to carry her own burden.

The best frame for negotiations is to place the burden of anxiety on the other party. It is in a female's nature to comply to strong frame. If a man asks for a blowjob, he will destroy his own power of negotiation. But if a man directs a female to the floor and pulls out his cock to be sucked, he will get more blowjobs than the man who asks. Silent consent is a man's assumption of authority and allows a female to shrug accountability for the sexual acts. When a man expects a female to verbalize consent, he wants a female to share responsibility for the sex. But a man who initiates with silent consent is a man who takes full responsibility for the sex act and allows a woman to fall into her frame of submission.

The more a man tries to have an open discussion on his sexual desires, the more the man shares responsibility for his desires with his woman. When a woman must verbally say "yes" to a man's sexual cravings, she controls a man to share moral doubt over his own urges. Women innately understand that verbal consent is a subtle way to share accountability for the act. For example, if a man said "I want to do this naughty thing… would you want to do that?" Think about the woman's feeling during this. She will think "I do want to do that dirty thing but I do not want him to think I do because he would think I am dirty. Also, him asking if I want to do it makes me think he has anxiety about doing it and wants validation over his own desires. It could just be easier for me to say that I do not do that kind of thing. It will reject him but at least he will think I am a good girl. Also, I wished he would just do the naughty thing so I could get the pleasure and he could take all the responsibility for it."

What a man must realize is that verbal consent is a bad negotiation tactic as well as placing a high amount of moral pressure on a female who does not want to come off as dirty in open agreement. And that asking for sex or a specific sexual act is the weakest approach which makes a female become unaroused not just by shared accountability but also from the weakness itself projected from the man.

Surrender

to

what

is

above

A female in sexual selection is looking for a masculine leader she can feel safe to submit to. The male must reassure the female's innate anxiety about reality which is based on her reproductive anxiety. All women hold tremendous reproductive anxiety. When the males in civilization become weak, the females will hold great anxiety over their reproductive access because they fear raising the children alone. Anxiety comes from fear of the unknown. Our anxiety rises when we know that a problem exists that holds unknown outcomes. A female is designed to hold tremendous anxiety about life from her own anxiety over her body.

The undecisive nature and uncertainty she holds over her body transfers to her psychology where it inspires doubt about creating another uncertain life in this uncertain world. Her weak sense of self makes her feel like a ship wreck survivor who clings to the wreckage in the wide-open waters. Water itself is symbolic of feminine nature and chaos. Fluid and unformed like water spreading over a flat surface. But a woman is not absolute in her chaos. She clings to the weak sense of self that partially contains her fluid nature. This is like the floating survivor who clings to the wreckage. When a female spots a framed man, he becomes like a sailing vessel near her struggling body in the open sea. A strong independent female is surviving, not thriving. This type of woman clings to the wreckage and has made it like a raft on the rough currents of her life. Remember, a "strong and independent" female is one who thinks about taking care of herself and not providing for a man. Her self-made raft is only built to secure and save herself which is perfectly represented by Rose on the door of the Titanic while Jack froze to death in the icy waters. What a man must realize is that women are looking to be saved. They are *looking for hands to reach down to them and not reach up to them*. They are looking up and not looking below. The fundamental reason for this is that a female innately understands that she is a biological dependent while carrying a child in womb. She depends on a male to provide/protect while she is incapacitated. But let us break down the "reach down" aspect to a female's own desire. To reach down is to be condescending to what is below. A female is looking for a man to lead her to salvation. This is why females look for strong egos in men because these men are condescending. These men look down on others because they view themselves as superior or "above" them. Remember, the hand of salvation must reach down to save.

The core reason a woman wants to be "saved" by a man is because she wants to surrender herself to him. She wants to cling to him and not the raft of her own making. She wants to let go of the wreckage of her own independence and fall into the arms of her hero. *She wants to abandon the weak sense of self she is clinging to and to share her man's sense of self*. This is the key. Women look for proud men because they too want to be proud. Women look for confident men because they too want to be confident. Women look for a strong sense of self in men because they want to share that same feeling. A man's world is his vessel which carries him through life. His world is a symbolic representation of his self-esteem. The male is object focused from the beginning which makes him future focused. He exists like a tall ship on the sea that can see from horizon (past) to horizon (future.) The female exists in the momentary pleasures of her indulgence like a raft being carried with the currents of the water. This is why women seek out men with strong ambitions because they want to join these men in their planned journey into future bounties. A woman wants to be saved by a man. He exists above not only her but life itself. He glides over the chaos like a captain on a ship. He brings her up to him and does not go down to her level. This is the difference between bad boys and nice guys. Nice guys will try to get on the female's level as a way to relate to them but what they are doing is abandoning their ship for a raft. The bad boy never leaves his ship, he invites the female aboard. To condescend is to stay above but to reach down.

This takes us to sex.

The act of sex should be a ritual of male belief. The man leads and directs a female through his desires. He reaches down to her and takes her on his journey. A man must be certain enough of his own reality to reassure a female that she can let go of her own. Women like men who lead dates because it is roleplay to the surrender of self for submission to the will of another. The male ego who does not let a female control him in social interactions is a precursor of a male who does not let her control him during sex. Remember, the core of a female's sexual pleasure can only be gained by her letting go of control. But what she truly is doing is letting go of her own weak sense of self to join the man's self. She must be willing to sacrifice the raft to join the ship. She must be willing to let go of her own struggling independence to rise up to the man of her desire. The key to a woman's sexual pleasure is in the release of her tight hold on her weak sense of self. A female who allows herself to dissolve into the self of her masculine leader will allow herself white hot pleasure. The darkness of her mind becomes white in heavenly light as the salvation from above pours down on her. It becomes an all-encompassing light of pure delight. There is no "her" only "him." Two become one flesh. The penetrator takes possession. For a brief moment there is no self to cling to or defend. Absolute submission which brings extasy. The man has reached down and taken a hold of the woman who was drifting on chaos. This is the truth of female passion that a "strong and independent" woman will never know. She lacks the faith in surrender to achieve the transformation. She lacks belief in what is beyond her and so she will never know anything outside her miserly grip.

Freedom from doubt

A female holds high amount of doubt about her body. This is because women innately understand that they are dependent on the objective male gaze for external validation over their own value in sexual selection. Women will deny this and will complain about the male gaze while reasoning that they work on their beauty for their own benefit and not the benefit of men. They shine themselves for not all men but only a few like a jeweler who showcases diamonds for select clientele. A female from a young age will have a strong desire for male attention and when her body matures, she will notice and feel validated by the increase in attention. This will inflate her ego but at the same time makes her fragile to the loss of attention or the criticism of her fragile sense of beauty.

While compliments inflate our ego and can feel good, they can also make us dependent on the opinion of others. This is the crux of a female's psychology in sexual selection. She has become dependent on the external male gaze which artificially puffs up her sense of self until the gaze is removed or dismisses her. When I say a female has a "weak sense of self" what this means is that a female is more reliant on the opinion of others to validate herself. She uses others as a way for emotional regulation. This is why women are inherently collectivist which makes their individual sense of self weak. And why a female romanticizes "finding herself" because she is perpetually confused about who she genuinely is. She holds tightly to others socially because she guides herself based on the will of others. Women are like the blind leading the blind. The male gaze is their greatest enemy and their most dear friend. They war against what is foreign to their own personal experience. The objective male eye. An eye that deems them worthy of sexual attention or casts them away as undesirable. The eyes of a king who passes them over for another. They curse his eyes and all men when they are made to feel invisible by what cannot see them. They look in the mirror and examine themselves closely to what the male eye sees and what is ignores. They examine the visible females and what form they have so as to form themselves into the same design. Or they indulge themselves in fatty delights, curse the desire of the select few men they truly want and settle for the desperate horde of male suitors they would otherwise ignore. These women will mock attractive females and the male gaze that forms them only because they are left in the darkness of their frustration.

The high uncertainty of self that comes from a female's blindness to her own genitalia and the mysterious blood horror that expels from her at the dawn of her womanhood both heighten her own body dysmorphia which is further made sensitive by her understanding that her single burden of performance is through the form and fading youth of her body. This causes a female to fall into high self-consciousness as her body becomes a prison of the male gaze and of her own biological imperative to sacrifice it for reproduction. And this takes us to the sex act with its naked vulnerability.

Both sexes disrobe of their civilized coverings and expose their bare animal forms.

This brings high amount of anxiety as clothes have represented a hiding of shame since the dawn of time. A shame in being exposed as just another creature in similarity to other mammals with male and female sex organs. A shame in the surrender of the body into animal passions. This is why a lot of men have anxiety over showing not only their naked body but also in breaking away from the missionary position with its high animal denial. A denial based on anxiety over the shame of falling into base desires. The female who already holds tremendous body anxiety will only be further thrust into self-consciousness with a male who drags his own body anxiety into the bedroom. This is the fundamental reason why women look for confident men with leadership skills. They want to be proudly led through the sex act with a man who holds no sex anxiety. Also, females are reassured by men who are not anxious over body functions which calms their own body anxiety. A man who farts in front of his female is in fact reassuring her of that body shame. His gross acceptance of his functions allows her to hide behind the display in her own feminine body denial. She remains ladylike only because the man allows her to hide behind his public display of indecency. The sex act itself holds an intimate display of indecency that would bring public shame. We hold collective shame over the sex act as a species because it is considered a gross function of our primitive desires. And so, we lock ourselves away in privacy to perform the heat of our indecent passions.

Now place a woman who is already sensitive about her body into this ritual of indecency and she will be cast into herself beyond barrier over barrier of intellectual denial. But that is not all. A female must be protective of her sexuality from its steep biological consequences. She must guard her sexuality from surrounding horde of males and feel safe enough to let go of that guard for a select male. This is the first barrier she lets down as she accepts the invitation to sex. But there is also the guard of shame over the sex act that she must let down as well as the barrier of her innate low self-esteem over her body. This is why a male must display confidence in the sex act and reassure the female that he holds no anxiety over his own performance. He must show her that he holds no anxiety over his own body and that she does not need to hold anxiety over her own naked body. He must show her that there is no reason to feel shame or guilt over animal imitations in positioning. He must show his strong desire by his own appreciation of her body which is the external validation she needs to feel comfortable in the act. This is why the visual objectification of the male gaze culminates with touch to reassure the female that the eye first appreciates what the hand seeks to touch. And the hand stimulates the single erogenous zone of the female form. Skin upon skin. The collapsing of borders and boundaries for the unification of flesh. The foreplay of intermingled bodies where the female surrenders her body to the penetrator. It is the man's responsibility to bring a woman out of herself and into his own possession. This is the place where female passion resides. It is in the external object of another that a female holds as most holy in her own socialization. She must be provoked in a trusting way to escape herself and to join the male as one. The man helps her to leap from her own self-consciousness into the certainty of his own consciousness. But she can only feel safe to join the man if he shows a brave example that lacks anxiety.

Walking the line

A man's sex anxiety comes from self-consciousness. But unlike the female who must be free to let go of herself completely, the male must exist in two worlds. He must both be above his animal passion as well as inside it. A woman is innately dual in nature and must learn to let go of both whereas a man is singular in nature and must learn to be dual. This can be compared to a hunter who must not only understand himself but the game he is seeking. To lead others, we must understand their minds while existing above their thoughts. A man must surrender himself to animal passion while being conscious enough to direct the experience. It takes a relaxed focus just as a tight rope walker must be relaxed while focused. What happens if a man begins to shake just thinking about walking a tight rope? His jangled nerves will not even let him step without failure onto the line he wishes to cross. This can be compared to the man who is too nervous to seek his bold pleasures in the sex act. He stumbles over the thought of his desire. The nervous response collapses his intent into erectile dysfunction. The performance dies behind the curtain before it can reach the spotlight. He is too afraid to initiate the performance because his fear has shown him failure before attempt. This is when men cannot achieve an erection. They collapse themselves from fear. They are too much in their minds to reach their body. They are frozen and paralyzed by the thought of failure that the thought of success remains out of reach. This is not to say all erectile dysfunction is psychosomatic. Sometimes a man's own blood has become stagnant within him which causes circulatory issues. For example, a sedentary lifestyle or high blood pressure itself could be the reason a man's blood flow is weak in his cock. A man should be having a morning erection every day. This means that his body is healthy and that the problem with erectile dysfunction would be psychological rather than biological. He should see a doctor for diagnosis to possible deeper concern. If a man is not able to achieve a morning erection, then he could be having physiological issues to address. I would recommend that he perform daily cardio, go on long walks, stop drinking alcohol, eat healthier foods and try to get a full night's rest. Then see if this helps him to achieve morning erections. Once that is solved then we can move on to the psychological reasons for erectile dysfunction.

If a man has morning erections but cannot get an erection with a female could be performance anxiety. What a man must realize is that a female wants a brave performance from her man in sex. She wants him to be bold, assertive and dominant. She wants him to be calm in his own confidence. She wants him to teach her what it means to be dirty. This is a major reason why men who are biologically healthy have sexual issues. They are too afraid of seeking their own sexual pleasure because of possible rejection or judgment. A man should fantasize about a dirty thought he wants to act out with a female and see if it stirs him to erection. Just the thought of doing something that is "dirty" to a female can make a man aroused. I am not telling a man to do something specific for a reason. Each man has his own definition of what "dirty" means and it is based on his own erotic imagination. But most male sexuality can be aroused by so called rude or dominant sexual behaviorism towards a female. Even just "bossing a female" in sex can arouse a male from the playfulness of the power dynamic in dominance. Once the niceties are removed then a man can achieve an aroused passion free from the anxiety that keeps him in cowardice. It takes bravery to be "dirty" because it means a man must brave being judged for his own sexual desire and brave being rejected for that desire. But what a man must realize is that a female becomes aroused by a man's acts of bravery in sex.

Stress is another issue that can cause a man sexual issue. When a man is too busy worrying about the future or the past will keep him from being in the moment which is necessary for base pleasure. We must surrender to the moment to realize it's pleasure. This is true of eating, sleeping or having sex. When a man gets stuck in his mind, he will lose focus of his body. Let us go back to the tight rope walker example. The man who cannot get an erection from the start is like a man who is too nervous to step on the rope. His mind keeps him from bodily action like a deer in the headlights. But also, a man can lose an erection in the middle of sex from performance anxiety. This is like the tight rope walker who gets to the middle of the line and looks down only to lose his balance. The fear makes freezes him into self-consciousness that seizes him into its frozen grip. The relaxed focus shifts to a frozen blur as he loses the moment to the thought of future failure. Then that projected failure from the future comes sailing back to the moment in a self-fulfilled prophecy. This self-consciousness makes us feel lost and a man cannot afford to feel lost when he must be directing sex. A man must be able to lead not only his own arousal but also the arousal of the female. But this can be simplified by the female acting as object to the male fantasy which ends up fueling both arousals at once.

Before a man can succeed in his performance, he must be willing to fail. It is catastrophizing which makes a man become paralyzed in fear. This is true of a tight rope walker who looks down or a man who speaks before an audience. He must be willing to lose so that he may win. He must be willing to diminish the risk of failure so as to calm himself in the moment. "If I fail, I fail. SO, WHAT" is the cure to most performance anxiety. If a man loses an erection with a woman, he should not sweat it. It is what it is. Most women only react to a man's own reaction anyhow. This is why a man should never apologize about a failed performance but know when to call it off. There is always another attempt in a future that is waiting. This turns a high-risk fear from catastrophic thinking into a relaxed effort. And what a man must realize is that a failed effort in sex will be owned by the female if the man does not make a showy display of apology. The female will think "Was it me?" and so forth. If a man has not experienced erectile dysfunction whether prior to sex or during sex, he will before his life ends. A man's life is full of stress and fears which all affect our sexual performance. It is common which means we should not give it ownership over our attempts. Just roll with the punches and keep fighting the fine fight.

Feasting in confidence

All base pleasures are rooted in animal complex. This complex has the biggest impact on our behaviorism. We are either in fight, flight or freeze. Our sleep, our sex and our eating habits are linked to our innate reaction toward others and the world that surrounds us. In The Wall Speaks, I broke down each as Raging Bull (fight), Flighty Bird (flight) and Paralyzed Deer (freeze.) The two that have the biggest negative impacts on sexuality are those that hide from confrontation. Let us breakdown what it means to be in flight or freeze in regards to sexuality. To get a better understanding of sex, let us focus on eating. All base pleasures are more tied together than most think. If an animal is eating quickly, it comes not just from greed but in the anxiety of its food being taken away from it. Animals will eat fast when they hold "feast fear." The anxiety of having the food removed or being forced off the food will make an animal eat in flight mode. When a creature moves through its environment fast and eats fast is a sign that the creature is trying to secure resource or preserve itself from danger. If a man is used to eating fast, walking fast and talking fast, he is in a fear state. A man will eat fast because he is unconsciously afraid of his food being taken away. A man will talk fast because he is unconsciously afraid of being interrupted. A man will walk fast because it is a defense mechanism against surrounding predators. This is like a boy running home from school because he is being preyed upon by violent bullies. All of these anxious behaviors can influence a man's own sexuality. How? His flight mode will make him prematurely ejaculate. He will think that he must impregnate the female as quickly as possible before he is moved off her by a stronger male. It is an unconscious reproductive fear. He is trying to quickly preserve his biological legacy before he is killed or before his female is taken away from him. This is one component to premature ejaculation. Another is that a man is highly sensitive to external stimuli from that same flight mode anxiety.

Think about it like a prey animal whose heart begins to beat in rapid rhythms only from the touch of a predator. A rabbit or a mouse's heart beat will thump in high fear from the stimuli from unfamiliar touch. The man who has premature ejaculation in sex will be overwhelmed by the touch, sound and visual of the female as his system goes into overload. The weakness from this state is that the man's nervous system is in imitation of small prey and the flight mode makes him ejaculate from that state of anxiety.

A man in flight mode will be easy to arouse and easy to orgasm. He is like a Flighty Bird that must descend quickly for food only to be scared away when others approach. This is the fundamental reason why anxious behaviorism in a male turns off a female. She is unconsciously thinking "This man is in flight-mode, he would quickly try to impregnate me and then be scared off by a stronger male." But not only that. Remember, anxious behaviorism is like injured splashes in the water that attracts predators. The more anxiety a man projects, the more he will be seen as in fear and therefore easy prey to those seeking it. This is why a female will become highly anxious with an anxious man. She knows innately that he is attracting predators to himself.

The man in freeze mode is like a paralyzed deer before headlights. The external stimuli make his sense of self collapse as he surrenders his consciousness to the fear before him. This is a man who creates splashy movements with other men in flight mode which attracts them as predators to himself. A major reason that paralyzed deer archetypes are high in intelligence. They are passive voyeurs to reality which causes them to become sensitive observers to the failures and success of others. While they are wise enough not to make splashes in the water to attract predators, their main strategy is in playing dead which causes them to lose opportunities to secure resource. The roleplay of death robs them of all opportunity of life. Unlike the flighty bird type that eats in anxious fear, the paralyzed deer will forsake food itself. This is what truly makes him safe from the predators. He opts out of competition completely which causes a false safety. When a man is in freeze mode under stress, he will lose his appetite in base pleasure rather than greedily indulge in them. The high stress will cause him to fast in not only food but also sex when the fear overwhelms him. This man's body will shut down rather go into flight. His biological defense to feasting is in the passive watching of others eat before him. He saves himself for another day by not competing with others and saves himself from conflict by his own lack of threatening presence. He watches the raging bull and the flighty bird in conflict and makes a choice to avoid all conflict to preserve himself. This type of man's body has been conditioned to shut down under duress.

He will easily lose appetite not only with food but also sex. Just as a deer becomes paralyzed from the headlights of a car, a man who has stage fright will become frozen in fear as he loses all sense of himself. His body will shut down from the overwhelming fear of the eyes of those who see through his cloak of invisibility. This type of man will have high amount of performance anxiety because being watched pulls him out of his survival method of anonymity. But unlike the performance anxiety that causes a flighty bird to become aroused into premature ejaculation, the paralyzed deer will struggle to become aroused and will easily lose arousal during the sex act. Remember, his body has been conditioned to shut down during stress and becomes self-aware during performance that triggers the self-consciousness which is the forgetting of self. He is used to being imprisoned by his own body and has learned to over intellectualize his base pleasures. This is all from the cowardice of action itself that he fears pursuing which cause him to fall into inaction as a survival method. The paralyzed deer type man kills his own sexual arousal to signal that he is not a threat to others who want sexual access to his female. His main strategy for survival is not greedily taking but rather in giving over his resource without a fight. The "headlights" that cause him to become self-conscious is a stress trigger which makes him intellectualize away from the sex act itself.

Whether a man is in flight or freeze, he will be holding high reproductive fear that will affect his performance during sex. Before a man can solve his own sexual problem, he must learn to conquer his root fear outside the sex act. But remember, all things in realty have sexual meaning. How fast a man eats, how fast he walks and whether or not he is afraid of confrontation all have sexual meaning. This is a major reason why females are highly sensitive to male behaviorism before they agree to sex.

All of a man's behaviors outside the bedroom are signals to his behaviorism within the bedroom. This is what a man must realize to improve his own sex life. He must solve conquering his fears and overcoming his anxiety in life to improve his sexual performance.

Think about sex on the most basic level to what it means. A female must feel safe to allow a man to impregnate her and she is reassured by his low sex anxiety for that propagation. She craves a calm man who is not afraid of death during the sex act. The sex act is an act of life and the man who brings fear, brings the smell of death to the life ritual. But what a man must realize is that his own death fear is unconscious to his animal complex of fight, flight and freeze. When a man overcomes that fundamental anxiety in his behaviorism will reassure his female that they are both safe during the sex act. She wants to follow the lead of her masculine penetrator. It is his calm and confident performance during sex that allows her the necessary feeling of safety to not only be submissive but to let go enough for her own pleasure.

Closing the gap

The heat of desire in a female's body is the anticipation of touch yet received. She is one single erogenous zone that is sensitive to the surrounding climate. Her body is "in touch" with the environment from its hyper sensitivity. The mystery of her sexual organ expands out over her in entirety. Her mind has been conditioned to be in wait of the revelation of mystery. This is the ultimate tease to her sexual pleasure. The possibilities of what could happen and where she will be led. Her sex is in waiting for direction to unknown destinations. When a woman is touched by a man, she can feel it across her whole being. When a woman is eyed by a man from afar, she is lost in her imagination over what his touch may feel like. This is why females are ultra-sensitive to the leering eyes and unwanted touches of men. They do not want to be possessed by unwanted advances. The gaze of an attractive man can send a *shudder of excitement* through a female while the gaze of an unattractive man can send a *shudder of repulsion*. What a man must realize is that there is energy in the space between two objects. The shudder is already there inside a woman but becomes either pleasurable or unpleasurable dependent on how the man reassures or incites female reproductive anxiety.

When a man is with a woman, she will be sensitive not only to what he does but also what he does not do. Her mind is racing about the possibilities of his desire being fulfilled by his touch. The air itself that surrounds a woman will be electrified over the possibilities of sex. This is why a framed countenance on a man acts as sexual roleplay. A female can feel the energy in a man's own restraint which builds arousal across her body. Women do not just pine for men in a physical absence but also pine for men who act framed in their presence.

When a man places his hand on a woman's leg or gently touches her hair can send a thunderbolt through her body and arouse her genitalia. The body of a female must be teased properly to build her erotic tension. Touch itself builds and breaks erotic tension. Build and release. This is why a man can build such an amount of erotic tension in a woman's body where she is thinking "take me already." She is wanting a release to the erotic build. The male uses his visual gaze to build his own arousal whereas a female uses her imagination (lack of visual) to build her own arousal. This takes us to the fundamental biological conditioning of a male's clear objective focus on his sexual organ and the female's lack of focus on her own which makes her reliant on imagination. When the man catches sight of a female, he approaches her to incite her imagination and the two harmonize together by touch. It is touch that creates a bridge between what is seen and what is unseen. The female captures a male's sight while the male captures the female's imagination and it is through touch that they fuel and relieve each.

In the sex act, a man will gain tremendous sexual heat with his eyes looking upon the female body while the female becomes aroused by the surrender of her objective mind for one of pure touch fueled by the anticipation and provocation of her imagination.

Females will not admit to enjoying the male gaze only because the gaze in majority is from unwanted males. But the male gaze itself from a rare male validates a female's sexual value and causes her to imagine sexual possibilities along with the male who is looking at her. The female is in the dark of herself from biological conditioning which makes her dependent on the gaze of a male to discern her own sexuality. This is why a young woman who is maturing in her body will begin to feel validated by the male gaze which causes her to begin to play with aesthetic beauty to further draw the gaze to her. She will spend countless hours before the mirror in imagining what the male gaze sees so as to further entice it to her form. The vanity of a female is based on her trying to get in the mind of the rare male gaze she wants to attract. Her time spent before a mirror is roleplay to the innate objective gaze of males. She wants to see what the man of her dreams sees. She wants to cure her inherent blindness and so trains herself in objective sight.

The mirror fascination of a female is based on her innate biological blindness and her reliance on the male gaze for her own sexual selection. What does a man see and how can I attract his eye? This is the unconscious rules in her mind that leads her to body flaunting, mirror gazing and face painting. All of this is to build erotic tension in males. But the irritating reality for a female is that it also attracts the majority of disgusting males that surround her. When women say "I hate how men leer at me," what they are saying is that they hate how their sexual strategy to get the attention of a few select males is also attracting unattractive males. They resent that the erotic tension their appearance gives off when it attracts males who do not deserve reproductive access. And this makes their imagination conceive of possible creep touches that could lead to unwanted pregnancies that would deform their bodies which thereby would make them unrousing for the few select men they are wanting to attract. How dare these creeps look at them. See? The females are triggering the male gaze but the unwanted male gaze is triggering the female's imagination. The fundamental fear of a female in sexual selection is rape. And it is the male gaze that triggers this primordial fear of bearing an unwanted child of an inferior male.

Now let us to go to the positive aspect of the male gaze. When a female is attracted to a man, she will want to be embraced by his gaze. She wants him to appreciate her beauty because she knows that he will arouse enough for propagation. This is a precursor reassurance to him being able to perform the sex act. If a man is not aroused by a woman's body, it will signal that the lack of sexual arousal could cause erectile dysfunction. This is why while a woman will say that she does not want to be a sexual object for men is true, the ultimate truth is she wants to be a sexual object for rare men. She knows her body must incite sexual passion in the rare man she wants to impregnate her. Both a man and a woman understand that the sexual energy exists without touch or speech. They understand that they both can feel a sexual heat and arousal simply from sight alone. The male gaze not only captures the female in its sight but also it captures by the female who presents herself to be seen as a sexual possibility. They both become one in that possibility with the man plotting his objective mission while the woman waits in passive excitement over the mystery of the man's intent.

The male gaze is sexual energy for both even if women hate to admit it. But what a man must realize about the male gaze is that it is the key to arousal while being at the same time a signal for desperation which destroys a female's arousal. This is why a brief look from a man to a woman can capture sexual energy but when the male leers at the female, it shows a desperation which is based on anxiety. And anxiety is not sexy. When a man chooses a female because she "caught his eye", it is in the restraint of his eye that builds further arousal for her. When a man is on a date with a woman, he should make sure that she is looking at him more than he looks at her. His distracted eye projects sexual abundance and delates the female's ego which is used to sexual thirst from men through their eyes. Remember, restraint is a tease and tease is foreplay. A man must be aroused by a female with his eyes without showing it.

A woman will war against the male gaze because of the sexual thirst from unwanted males but will mourn it when its gone. Why? Because if a woman cannot attract low value men, how can she attract high value men? See? This is why the most "strong independent" feminists will spend years complaining about the male gaze during their youth only to complain about not getting the male gaze when they get old. The surrounding horde of unwanted males who gaze do not signal true beauty in a female, but the surrounding unwanted males' disinterest does signal true ugliness. And this is why the male gaze is both a woman's worst enemy and her best friend.

Above the fear

One of the most puzzling aspects of female sexual psychology is when females seek out criminals in sex. The biggest criminals in our times, most prolific serial killers, will attract young and attractive female fan bases. These young women will seek out these dangerous figures from a morbid curiosity that verges on sexual excitement. Why are women attracted to bad boys and criminals? There are multiple reasons and we will break them down one by one. The first is that women are attracted to men who "play by their own rules." This means that a man is outside the existing paradigm and behaves as if he is in his own paradigm. All women inherently are obedient to existing rule structures and are submissive to the game that they were culturally brought up inside. This comes from not only the fact they are conditioned to be reliant on peer pressure to validate their uncertain emotionalism but also to the fact that as the more vulnerable sex, they are innately aware that survival comes from "fitting in" to environments. This is why a female will fall into a Stockholm syndrome where she normalizes herself to a threatening situation as a coping mechanism against her innate feelings of helplessness.

A major reason why women are attracted to bad boys and rebels is because these men symbolize a freedom from fitting in which overwhelms them. While a female is psychological imprisoned from peer pressure and social obligations, the criminal represents someone who is only beholden to self and is free of those suffocating burdens of socialization. The anti-social behavior of a criminal is seen as an act of freedom from the restraints of fake niceties that hold social communities together.

The selfishness of a male in sexual selection is viewed in a positive light by females because the females view themselves as benefiting from the greed of these potential protector/providers. They not only will share in the selfishly gained resources but also share in the freedom of the unrestrained identity. But let us digger deeper. What is the mind of a leader? It is someone who is more certain of their own reality than the perceived reality of their followers. The reason why a leader does not fraternize with his followers is not just that the mystery of his power increases respect but also that solitude allows him to perceive himself as uniquely separate from the group in order to lead them. A reason why Moses and Jesus Christ both fasted in solitude before assuming a new role as leader. This is symbolized as Moses going up the mountain to be alone with his thoughts. A separation of his thoughts from groupthink but also in order to see the group as small like ants below him. The symbolization of a king on a high throne or the leader on top of the pyramid of power hierarchy. To lead others, we must be above them in thought. This is why when a leader does not fraternize with his followers and when he is not easily controlled by their moral judgments, he is viewed as strong to the role he must play.

Women are attracted to criminals and even serial killers because these men trigger the desire of leadership in sexual selection even if it is confused. The most hardened criminal views himself above the law and above moral systems. He places himself as a "god" among men that is not bound by the same rules. This high degree of self-assurance and confidence becomes like a mojo scent that pulls a female into a man's orbit. But we can even dig deeper. To be above mankind is to not be confined by what they are confined by. And what is a female confined by? She is imprisoned by guilt and shame. Social shame is the biggest controllers and influencers of female psychology. This is why we see a rise of race and class guilt that is used to shame people into submission in our times. It is a common feminist tactic for power gain in using her own weakness against others.

The harden criminal archetype is a man who does not let social shame control him into submission and who feels little to no guilt over his own selfish behaviorism. A female wants to be possessed by a strong man's frame because she wants to identify herself with his own confidence. Women are sexually drawn to criminals because they want to identify with the freedom from shame and guilt that these types project. These men are not controlled by the common group dynamics that are suffocating to female psychology. These men give off key behavioral elements of leadership qualities that confuses women into arousal. But also, the hyper sensitivity of the female's body as erogenous zone makes them excited by the mere presence of danger and its possibility. This is why the female fan clubs that mob a serial killer are getting aroused by being in the same room of the killer in court proceedings. The playful aspect to danger can be likened to someone who wants to have a dangerous animal as pet. It is an imitate connection to a killing machine that chooses not to kill us. When a woman or man owns a tiger or lion, they are gaining intimacy in the mere fact that the dangerous beast has deemed them worthy of life. This is a major reason why women are attracted to erotic fiction of violent beasts where they see themselves as the one who can tame them. But more specifically, that the violent beast will show mercy to them even if it is not merciful to others which is interpreted as the deepest form of affection. It also is a major ego trip for the female. She becomes the one that truly understands the misunderstood beast while setting herself up as the savior who can tame it.

Another reason why a female can be attracted to a criminal type is that her expectations for a protector has become extreme and confused. For example, if a female comes from a violent home, was raised in a violent neighborhood or is escaping a violent relationship, her high anxiety over violence will make her seek out a violent man who can protect her from those fears. But what these women soon find out is that violent men who they rely on for protection soon become the perpetrators of the violence itself. It is the violence that eased their initial anxiety that ends up ultimately increases it in the end. The ancestral memory in females is one of death and rape. For thousands of years women have seen their sexual partners killed before them by stronger men and have been kidnapped into sexual slavery. Over and over. This is why a man's good intent will be lost to the reality of his capacity for violence. If a woman's protector falls in battle, then not only is she at risk to the wills of another but her own children will become at risk. This is why a female will not care about a man "standing up for her" in a violent confrontation if the man loses the fight and leaves her alone to fend for herself. She does not need a man with good intentions but rather a man who is capable of winning the threatened situations.

Some women are attracted to killers because these men are seen as successful in the ultimate truth of reality. Violent combat. They have broken the most guilt-ridden rule known to mankind, murder. The unconscious collective memory of females is that of good intentions dying on the battlefield. A man may be a "good husband" or "good father" but if he is lying dead then he is good for no one. This is the cold reality of existence that women are innately aware of even if they will never admit to it. The one who lives is the one who can afford to have good intentions. When females flock around criminals and killers they are flocking around the eternal wisdom of life over death. They are flocking around those who hold the power of life and death in their hands. The executioners of their own judgment systems. The victors by sheer brutality in sexual selection. A cold embrace of a forgotten truth that lies dormant in the blood-soaked memory of their ancestors.

What a woman wants

Since a female is the physically weaker and more vulnerable sex of our species, she must rely on her wits to gain advantage. Women innately understand that a physically larger male can be easily controlled through emotional gaslighting. A man can be a giant but will surrender this authority to a woman. In fact, a lot of women in our times control men through guilt and shame tactics. What a man must realize is that unconditional love only exists with our mothers. And the only reason why they have unconditional love is because they see themselves through their own genetic legacy. A mother who loves her child unconditionally is in actuality loving herself unconditionally. The truth of all organisms on earth is that they are in eternal conflict with each other for supremacy. This is not to say that conflict is a negative. For example, a female is designed to test a man's authority to reassure her own reproductive anxiety which also strengthens a man's authority from the challenge itself. And the great burden of performance the females of our species place on males, the stronger males become to meet those demands. Remember, it is women who create male supremacy by the burden of performance they place on men. But absolute power corrupts absolutely. The corruption of holding too much power creates a disharmony between leader/follower which causes chaos. When someone abuses their power, what they are doing is acting in greed over their advantage which inspires resentment over their tyranny. Kings fall this way in revolutions just as husbands lose control over their families. The hand that holds too tightly to power loses its grip. The greed is a sign of anxiety just as an animal eating in fear. It is a short-term indulgence in the moment because of a fear losing control and resources.

How does this apply to sex? In our times of female dominance, we see a rise of the burden of performance that women place on men while shrugging all performance on their side. A female in a place of power will be free to place high demands on what she expects from a man in sexual selection. But if a man openly discusses his own demands in sexual selection, it is seen as preposterous. The man is even shamed for having any standard in sexual selection with women. Women in our times can say "I want a man who makes more money, taller, successful, ambitious, physically fit, has all his hair" spoken without shame. What is the response to this high expectation and standard that women place on men? "Get the best deal you can," "you go girl," etc., etc.

A woman is not shamed for her own high expectations that she places on men in sexual selection. Why? Because that level of arrogance comes from the corruption of too much power. This is what men must realize in our times. Women are encouraged to be greedy in sexual selection for the absolute best deal they can get while at the same time shaming men for having any burden of performance for them. Do women encourage each other to blindly pursue love in sexual selection? No, of course not. A female is looking for a protector/provider who can ease her reproductive anxiety enough for her to feel safe in pregnancy. She has a long list of conditions that a man must fulfil before she becomes emotionally attached to him. Note that. A woman's love is conditional. If a man fails to meet the high burden of performance in sexual selection, a woman will magically fall out of love with him. If a man does not meet the burden of performance from the start, he will not even be seen by women. His failure to meet conditions will make him invisible in sexual selection. But remember, a female's greatest power is through emotional manipulations. A woman can make a man believe that his love must be unconditional while her love is highly conditional. This is why women can freely talk about the burden of performance they expect from men while shaming a man for even saying he has one single expectation for a woman. And what is most emotionally hurtful to women? The truth. This is the same for us all. It is the truth that most hurts us because it reveals something beyond us. When a man is attracted to a young and attractive female, what he is attracted to her health and fertility. Two things that majorly damage a woman's fertility is age and obesity. It is common for morbidly obese females to have fertility issues.

The truth of our species is that men are attracted to fertile women and women are attracted to men who can make them feel secure while bearing children. This is why a female's burden of performance that she places on a man falls into a mix of protector/provider while a man's burden he places on females is based on the appearance of fertility. This is the truth regardless if it hurts our feelings. This is the truth now and this will be the truth a thousand years from now. It is part of our design and nature. Remember, all psychology is built upon biological necessity. And this takes us to the modern arrogance that comes from females in sexual selection. The obesity epidemic among women is a form of dominance and a shrug of their own sexual burden. Do women get shamed for their expectations of men being tall, fit and wealthy? No. But if a man expects a woman to be fit, he is publicly shamed. If fact, at the peak of modern feminism, there is something that women are pushing called "fat acceptance." What they are doing is trying to shrug one of the few aspects of their own fertility marker and burden of performance. This is a major reason why it is feminists who are pushing this agenda. And we know feminists only care about the very best deal they can get in sexual selection and how much power they can transfer from men to women.

Think about how arrogant it is for women to have high expectations for men and then think men should just be grateful for the opportunity to be with them regardless of how they look. Why do some men allow themselves to be gaslit into accepting this situation? They have tremendous low self-esteem, demonize themselves and moralize women. These types of men view women as angelic and deserving of unconditional love. This is while the women greedily expect them to fulfil their conditions. When a generation of men are taught to think less of themselves because of their own sex and are raised under the authority of their mothers, they will view all women as motherlike figures. We have an epidemic of relationships in our times where the sexual dynamic is mother/son. The men in these relationships want to believe that romantic love is unconditional because they want the same love that their mothers gave them. They allow women to hold steep conditions for romance while thinking it selfish to hold any condition. Women become emboldened over them, and that absolute power creates a Jezebel effect where the women increase their demands in greed. How do these women control their men? With shame and guilt tactics. These men are weak minded and easily fall prey to emotional manipulations. They are weak willed and readily sacrifice their dignity for any opportunity for sexual access. And so, their women hold the possibility of sex over their heads while mocking them. The women abuse their power because the men have given them too much power. It is as simple as that.

A female is not an angel no more than a man is an angel. We are human beings and each one of our sexes has different expectations in sexual selection. The fact that men cannot openly discuss the truth of their sexual expectations of fertility in females is proof that we live in a matriarchy where men are subservient to the open authority of women. This is why a man should not think it is unloving to place a burden of performance on a female in sex. The burden itself will counterbalance the burdens she places on the man which balances the power between the sexes. It cures the corruption of absolute power and heals the relationship. And this is truly an act of love.

Headless authority

The fact that females are the perpetrators of male supremacy by the burden of performance they place on men in sexual selection is one example why they do not understand the root design. For example, feminists will war against male supremacy, the patriarchy and inequality of the sexes while at the same time placing an inequal burden of performance on men they are seeking in sexual selection. They do not realize cause effect and fundamentally are confused about the means of production. A feminist will complain that the current system is set up to reward male achievement while ignoring female achievement but will be oblivious to the burden that informs all things in human civilization which is their decisions in sexual selection. The system is merely a reflection of our sexual selection and it is women themselves who decide the rules that shape that system.

Women have the biggest influence on the behaviorism of men by the burden of performance they place on men for sexual access. If women did not place such a high burden on men, we would not have a civilization. *The inequality that most perturbs women in the world is all a direct result of the steep inequality of the sexual burden they place on men.* An attractive woman will happily receive the attention of multiple male suitors who compete against each other for her interest but will then complain that the system of competition instead of cooperation in our world must change from its unfairness. But what makes a female ignorant is that she herself makes our sexual selection unfair based on the measure of competition she implements. Even the most ardent feminist who fights for equality between the sexes will expect a steep disparity between the burden she places on men in sexual selection compared to what they place on her. This feminist who proudly pursues a life of "strength and independence" will still look for a superior male in sexual selection who is taller, stronger, makes more money and has greater ambitions than her. She is rewarding male superiority with her own sexuality. And that sexual reward has not just an influence on her own romantic relationship but on all men and the entire system of things. This lack of understanding of the root processes is inherent to female nature. It is a lack of rationality. Remember, to become rational we must not just ask "why?" but "why?" upon "why?" until we get to the root of our understanding. And each "why?" we ask removes a layer of warm illusion that comforts our emotional worldview. The deeper we go into the meaning of all things the more we must leave behind previous fantasies. For example, the idea that all romantic love is based on condition is unromantic and troublesome to an emotional worldview. The idea that all human existence is based on reproduction before death is unromantic and therefore upsetting to sensitive ideals. The emotional worldview keeps men and women from digging too deeply into the meaning behind their behaviorism and the behaviorism of others. This is why females are "headless" or lacking in rationality. A major reason that the major organized religions designated man as "head" over women and family. It takes cold rationality to grasp the past with one hand and the future with the other. It takes cold rationality to look upon the blood and guts that gives meaning to the shining skin over a body.

Women are innately confused about how things work and the means of production because it requires them to dispel themselves of their own emotional worldview which they refuse to let go of. A reason why feminists openly hate free enterprise while refusing to see that it is based on the competition in our sexual selection which they are responsible for. They refuse to understand that the equal distribution of goods does not work because the unfair distribution of sex motivates males into higher achievement which produces such goods. They war against inequality of performance between the sexes while being the key motivator of male performance itself by sexual reward.

The ignorance over the means of production can be seen even in the sexual behaviorism of feminists. It is common for feminist relationships to suffer from "dead bedroom." A major factor for this this is that sexual pleasure for female is based on her own willing surrender into submission which allows her a relaxed release of the reproductive guarding that she holds from sex anxiety. But what does a proud feminist do? She equalizes all power between herself and her man in a relationship which increases her dominant behavior in sex which keeps her guarded. But even in feminist relationships, women will try to have sex talks with their men about being more dominant in the bedroom. These women think that they can flip a switch on their own submission in sex and that this roleplay in the moment will allow them to reach their pleasure. But what they do not realize is that true submission in sex comes from trust in the authority outside the bedroom. This is why a man who acts as dominant with his woman in all situations keeps her in foreplay for when sex does happen. *Sex is everywhere in the house, not just the bedroom.* True submission cannot be just switched on for a brief moment and switched off when the moment is over. The reason is that a woman can only access the core of her own sexual pleasure through the trust of the male's leadership which allows her the trust needed to let go. The more a female trusts a man's authority in other aspects of their relationship, the more she will be conditioned to trust his authority in the sex act. This ignorance of the means of production of sex is the same as a woman's ignorance of the means of a man's success in sexual selection. There is a saying among men that women do not want to know what it takes for a man to win, she only wants to "wait at the finish line and reward the winners." What a man must realize about female nature is that a woman can only truly understand reality through her own means in sexual selection. And this means that she will view all things as being versus becoming. She expects things to simply be and does not realize what it means for things to become. Good sex needs to just happen just as a prized man needs to just appear before her.

Once a man understands what I am teaching him, he will see that all the biggest issues that feminists fight for are inherently ignorant of the root of the issues they battle. It could be a policing issue in a city. Women will focus on the most superficial aspect like race hatred without realizing that police tend to focus on fatherless neighborhoods. That fatherlessness and matriarchal conditioning the giant determining factors in criminal behaviorism. That fatherlessness increases the chances that a boy will use drugs, join a gang and have unprotected sex. This chaos from matriarchal communities itself attracts police attention and not the race of the inhabitants. Why would feminists ignore the means of this production? Because the asking of why, why, why will take them to a cold reason that conflicts with their ego and emotional worldview. They want to believe that "they do not need a man" and that they are "enough" which means that single mothers are more than enough for child raising. Since the root of the issue cannot be addressed, they choose a being over becoming reason which is race over psychology. It becomes born this way and not raised this way. What this means at the heart of the matter is that women are horrible problem solvers because of their willful ignorance over the root cause of the issues they want to solve. And the reason why women are horrible problem solvers is because they do not need to learn to solve the problem of their own sexual deprivation. A man must fail over and over in sexual selection. He must adapt himself to the world that is rejecting him. He must apply true humility in knowing the truth of why he fails with women regardless of his feelings. This basis for men being able to solve problems with rationality comes from the fact that we must solve the fundamental issue of being sexless. The major difference between a male and female is that a female does not hold the same level of sexual desperation that motivates the male into problem solving because she merely needs to present and surrender herself to the right male to solve her own sexlessness.

Sexual humiliations

The world is in eternal conflict. The poor get poorer and the rich get richer. The large eat the small and the weak are preyed upon by the strong. This is masculine frame. This is the fundamental truth that most offends women and their emotional worldview. It is cold and unforgiving. I learned from a young age what being a sexual threat means in life. A boy who is half blood to siblings or adopted will be unconsciously seen as a sexual threat and will be treated as outsider. All men hold some sexual anxiety over other males but men who are separated by blood will hold even more sexual anxiety. This sexual anxiety will be heightened in mixed families where step fathers, half siblings and step siblings must coexist. Growing up, I was raised along with half siblings where we shared a mother but had different fathers. I was the lone child from my father and mother which meant that I was unconsciously viewed as a product of our mother's cucking of my siblings' father. This caused an innately hostility and over compensation manage the hostility from that sex anxiety. When a boy is truly genetically alone in a shared litter, he will be treated as outsider regardless of conscious thinking. This meant that I was the symbol of a theft of not only the previous position of "baby" from my mom's previous litter but also a living symbol of the sexual threat of my own father.

My older brother would make an effort to diminish my sexual confidence with public humiliations and would play jealous games between us and our mother. This is not to say that my brother does not love me or that I do not love him, the point of this is to show unconscious animal behaviorism in sexual selection. But he without doubt would single me out for emasculations. Constant teasing and testing of my sexual confidence. There was without a doubt in my mind a sexual insecurity between us. But I also realized that the more he would attack me before women, the more the women viewed it acts of sexual threat which only gave me power. Women are more aware of men showing sexual insecurity than men themselves. While I was mixed blood which is an inherent threat, this sometimes can occur even in brothers who share both parents. We call this a "pecking order" where an older brother will become domineering to his younger brother.

The establishment of a pecking order is that the older sibling fears losing sexual dominion over his younger sibling. When an older brother bullies his younger brother, what he is doing is reaffirming his authority over the younger one with physical and psychological warfare. But at the root of this behaviorism is sexual anxiety that causes the older to condition the younger into a state of submission. The older male is wanting to secure increased sexual access with females and this means he will try to emasculate and subjugate his younger brothers. This behaviorism is more overt in mixed litters where fathers are different. A reason for this is that the new father sexually humiliates the previous father by his sex with the mother. And any children that come from that new union will be living symbols of cuckoldry. There was always a tremendous amount of sexual anxiety during my youth from this situation. Not only was I a lone child from the union of my father and mother, but also this mixed litter was raised with a step-father which added a further sex anxiety to the upbringing. All dominant behaviorism between males is based on sexual selection. This unique upbringing allowed me to study sexual anxiety and to discern what made myself a sexual threat to others from my outsider role. My fatherless childhood conditioned me into a Machiavellian outlook on existence from the reality of other's cold animal behaviorism. This is usually why orphans will become hardened into cold survivalism where they feel zero guilt in psychological manipulations for their own gain. It is from being forced to be closer to the animal of our sexual selection where they must experience being seen as a heightened threat to other men.

Biological fathers are incredibly important to a boy's psychology for the reason that it is a rare circumstance where a male shares sexual power dynamics with another male. When a boy is viewed a sexual threat from being fatherless or being raised in a mixed litter, he will see clearly the threat that he has on his environment and what other males view as holy to their own dignity, their sexual pride. We have countless examples in our times of males emasculating other males to make themselves feel sexually dominant. They belittle those they view as a threat as a showy display of prowess. Have you ever been sexual humiliated, emasculated or bullied by other men? Remember, they are letting their animals escape the cage and are being controlled by unconscious instinct for sexual access before they die. But what you should never forget is that to be seen as a threat is to be seen as a usurper to power. And that is a blessing in disguise. It is our hidden potential that causes the most fear in those who are afraid of losing their own authority to another. Being an outsider has been a curse wrapped in a blessing. A blessing that is brighter than the heat from hell's torment. I am who I am from what I have experienced. I am how I am from every single failure and challenge in my life. Recognize each act of persecution as love. Recognize those who prey upon our weaknesses as magnifying lenses on a weakness we must fix. Only strength matters. Only the will to survive will carry us to the grave. Do not curse those who torment. Do not curse those who emasculate. They are unconscious animals who we must battle in order to gain strength from their attacks. How can someone slay a dragon that feeds on each attack? How can someone stab at what eats blades? Do not fear the conflict but let it nourish you in battle. Remember that a man has himself and that is more than enough. Everyone in a man's life is preparing him for the throne he must ascend to. Turn doubt into belief. Figure out what others fear and overcome it. Overcome them all. Become something proud.

Freedom from monogamy

The rise of careerism among women in civilization in our times is fundamentally about a woman's discontent with the majority of male options in sexual selection. Remember, a female is looking for a protector/provider in sex because it reassures her reproductive anxiety. There will always be a great discontent among women in a monogamous society for the reason most males are unattractive in the selection of our species. Women wanted the freedom to make money as a way to gain independence from unattractive males who they relied on as providers. What is the strategy of females in sex? They present themselves to males and make themselves available for approach. But in times where the majority of men were providers for their females, the females were confined to the nest for child rearing and not able to present themselves to other men. When women were fighting to enter the work force many years ago, what they were doing was fighting for opportunity to cuck their weak male providers.

What a man must realize about females is that all of their behavior is based on sex anxiety just as all our own behaviorism is based on sex anxiety. The anxiety in the vast unhappiness of women in this world comes from reproductive anxiety with their male partners. It was this great anxiety that motivated women to take to the streets for financial independence and political power. Female empowerment was driven by financial freedom because the ultimate way genetically inferior and psychological unframed men control women is through financial dependence. It was through the control of money that infantilized females into a state of submission where they were forced to rely on provider males for survival.

The female empowerment movement was an escape from the tyranny of monogamous arrangements with the majority of males. The rise of sexless men in our time is a direct result of woman's liberation. We have a great many "incels" because these men no longer have the financial power over females that once stabilized monogamy. Monogamy itself is an institution that most benefits men as it allows an equalized distribution of sex among men. This allows a baby boom as normally these men would not have sexual access. The sexless males of our current generation no longer have physical access to women but rather must surrender their desires to digital access as females still use the genetically inferior males as providers without having to reproduce with them.

When females can exploit men that they no longer have to be reproduced with while still using them as providers allows these females to make themselves sexually available to the few males that they truly want to impregnate them. The "career woman" is a female who attempts to be free from the reproductive fear of being burdened with inferior seed. While the career woman wants to rise in financial wealth as a way to break free from marriage to inferior men, she also rises up the corporate ladder as a way to make herself available to powerful men. But just like all female problem solving, it ignores the root cause of her behaviorism while ultimately causing her and the world more suffering. Why? The financial wealth that career women seek in order to be free of inferior providers has no benefit to them in sexual selection unlike males. Men innately seek out careers and entrepreneurship so that they may provide for a female and family. Women seek out careers as an escape from the monogamous based family arrangement. It is women in the work place that most harms our sexual selection of our species. Why? Regardless of how much money a female makes, she is designed to look for a male who makes more money than she makes. With the rise of college educated career women in our civilization, we see a further separation between the sexes as men are increasingly seen as insufficient in their own burden of performance.

What moron feminists who ignore the means of production did not want to admit is that females will never want to provide for males in sexual selection. It is that base fact that makes a woman's career not a betterment of family and society but a pure act of selfish rebellion against monogamy itself. The more a man understands my teachings, the more he will begin to realize that women are the greatest enemies of what they publicly support. For example, women will spend all their time complaining about the unfairness of male supremacy while being the perpetrators of an unfair burden of performance they place on males that creates a male supremacy. This is the same with monogamy. A woman will complain about male promiscuity and wish for monogamy while at the same time destroying monogamy with her own sexual selection strategy.

Women's liberation was fundamentally a movement to destroy monogamy so that the majority of females could secure sexual access to the few males that they want to propagate with. Women will never admit to wanting to share a male in sexual selection while they readily share males in our selection. The same for women who only give nice guy advice for men in romance while seeking out the men who show opposite behaviorism to impregnate them. A woman is a dual creature. Her tongue moves one way and her feet move another. She is designed for hypocrisy because subterfuge most benefits her in a world of violent men. The feminine mystique casts a shadow screen of secret intent. But if a man looks closely at the biggest political issues women pursue, he will begin to see that it is all based on reproductive anxiety. That is the ultimate frame for their motivations. What issues? The basic provided needs from collective government assistance which is a fear of being without provider in marriage. The opening of borders which is an increasing of the genetic pool when males become viewed as inferior. The greatest political issue is abortion which is a hallmark of reproductive anxiety in giving birth without a secured protector/provider. Once a man's eyes open to the true animal behavior in a female they will never close again.

Women controlled by fear

When monogamy is destroyed by female liberation movements that dispossess a generation of males into sexlessness, this creates a major issue with sexual inequality. The only reason we have a rising number of virgin males and so called "incels" is because the burden of performance of females has skyrocketed in our times. There are three key things that females look for in sexual selection with males, protection (muscles), provider-ship (makes more money) and leadership skills. But the fundamental premise of the female liberation movement is to create financial independence in females who pursue high paying careers while teaching them leadership skills. This has empowered females in two aspects of expectations they place on males in our selection. Does this mean that women will only look for strong and muscular men who lack leadership skills in sex? No. *A woman never abandons her criteria for sexual selection, she increases her burden of performance beyond her own.* If a woman makes a lot of money, she will expect a man to make more, if a woman is conditioned for dominance by being taught leadership skills, she will look for a more dominant male to lead her. This is the root reason why in times past, young men were encouraged to be future world leaders. It was in alignment with our sexual selection to groom men into behaviorism that would benefit them in mating.

When a generation of females are conditioned for leadership and careerism, they are being conditioned into an even more narrow focus in sexual selection. These strong and independent females will feel that there are no good men nowadays because they have lifted themselves above all their suitors. What does this mean for sexual behaviorism in our times? It means we have a record number of sexless men who are deemed inferior for propagation by the majority of females. While women have always deemed the majority of males inferior, the problem has only gotten worse through female empowerment. The pool of desirable men has shrunk down to a few who most women jealously battle over. These men act like roosters in hen houses. They move from female to female to female as a generation of sexless men rot in the despair of their own decay.

In times past, the majority of males could marry a female, have sexual access and raise a family. Now in our times, men abandon reality for a fantasy of digital pleasures. These sexless men opt out of sexual competition that has been rigged against them for pornography and pixelized prostitutions. A rising amount of strong and independent females end up sharing the few protector males while they exploit the growing abundance of sexually desperate males as distant providers. This generation of feminists have demonized the male gaze while capitalizing upon it by showcasing their bodies to faraway fans who abandon touch for sight alone. The vast divide between males and females in our civilization has been caused by encouraging females to be our future leaders.

But this takes us to one of the most anxiety inducing problems that haunt modern women's minds. How do females navigate a world of sexless males? Remember, females do not want to have sex with these males and have a tremendous fear of being impregnated by them. This is why feminists encourage digital prostitution. They may not like the idea of these sexless males satisfying their animal heat alone in their homes but at least it allows these males to release their desires away from them. And males who satisfy their sexual heat with each other is another solution to the male problem. This is the fundamental reason why women and feminists have always made male homosexuality a main issue along with abortion. Both solve the issue of reproductive fear that women get when they believe males are too inferior for propagation. Remember, all a woman's political issues are based around her sex anxiety. And the fundamental issue that arises when women are freed from the imprisonment of monogamy with the majority of males is that it creates a massive increase in predatory males who leer at them in sexual desperation. This innate rape fear drives them to support all solutions to the sexless male problem.

All feminist support of male homosexuality comes from a celebration of these men making themselves sexually harmless to them. These males who are dispossessed from our sexual selection are applauded when they choose to redirect their animal heat to each other in fruitless pursuit. But it is a single solution for a dual issue. When men find it easier to have sex with each other than it is to have sex with females, they will eroticize that decision as empowerment. And when young boys are taught to demonize heterosexual men as the enemy, then they will identify themselves completely with the female sex as a way to empower themselves in this environment. We cannot stop the drive to power but only redirect it. If a young boy feels that he can escape social shame by eroticizing a change in his sexual behavior, it will compel him into this change. When we romanticize defeat and failure, we spare our egos. This is when a man will talk about being sexually attracted to obese females only because they are within his reach. Or when a man romanticizes simplicity only because he fears complexity. We all do this to varying degrees as ego defense. But what a man must realize is that the main agenda of females who gain power is to protect their reproductive rights. What this means is that women will tirelessly work to make sure that the majority of males do not reproduce.

A monogamous system that is usually seen in religious communities is when each male is paired off with a female which creates an equal distribution of reproduction. This is what true male empowerment looks like. This is what feminist deem "the patriarchy" when they discuss the times of oppression. There is no greater oppression for a female than to bear the child of a male she views as inferior to herself. The truth of female liberation is to be free from the socially arranged equalized pairing with males with females. Women innately know that only a few males deserve to reproduce while the rest deserve to have their genetic legacy end. But we can go even further in why females celebrate and obsess over male homosexuality. Females are innately reassured by male leadership. When homosexual men are pursuing fruitless sex with each other, women are reassured that they too can be fruitless by abandoning their reproductive anxiety. Not only do feminists celebrate homosexual men redirecting their male gaze and sexual heat to each other but they are also reassured that sex can remain fruitless to spare them from bearing children.

When females increase their social positions in society by increasing their wealth and power from leadership, they increase their reproductive anxiety. This is because the more power they get over men the more they are anxious to bear these men's children. We have an unprecedented level of sex anxiety in females in our times and that anxiety is being redirected to other areas. It is not a coincidence that feminists obsess over male homosexuality, abortion and climate change.

"But Jerr" a voice calls out from off the page "I understand that females celebrating homosexuality and abortion are both based on sex anxiety but why climate change?"

Because the fundamental solution that women are drawn to with climate change is that to solve the problem, we must produce less which includes having less children. See? Once a man understands the reality of female nature, he will begin to see it is all reproductive anxiety. This is why climate change has become a religious position among feminists. It has spared their egos and given meaning to the fruitlessness of their careerism. It gives meaning and morality to their reproductive anxiety. They have turned fear and selfishness into brave compassion. Climate change must mean the end of the world within their own generation so as to give meaning to their childlessness in that generation. The massive female empowerment across civilization over the past hundred years has made celebrated infertility the main agenda by female world leaders. This is why feminist parents are currently indoctrinating their children into homosexuality and transsexuality. Both are abandonments of heterosexual reproductivity of our species. When this generation awaken to the psychological castration that their parents forced upon them, they will become blind in rage.

What does it mean when parents teach their children that true empowerment comes from not being heterosexual? What does it mean when women celebrate heroes of reproductive death? The grand expression of bright color and jubilant joy of our times is a final scream into the abyss. It is a mad celebration of the greedy filled pleasures of the moment over the belief in tomorrow. The chant of the witch is "we are the final generation" the chant of the Jezebel spirit is "we are the final generation" the chant that is whispered into the ears of this fatherless age. Wake up. Women are ruled by a fear of reproduction and they are leading a world off a genetic cliff because they are too arrogant to admit the truth of that fear. All their politic is soaked in sex anxiety and so they lift of an entire generation to be sacrificed to mother nature to appease the fear that they refuse to face.

Islands
worlds
apart

Female liberation has freed women from the confinement of monogamy to undesirable males and created a vast divide between the sexes. No other time in mankind's history have we such levels of single females and single males unwilling to interact with each other. What a feminist and even some sexless men will refuse to admit is that the males and females in our species were meant to balance each other. There are two frames of viewing reality. Two mediums with two different messages. Two anatomies with two different destinies. The emotional worldview and the rational worldview. A worldview for nurturing within the nest with its heightened presence to the moment and sensitivity to the needs within. And then there is the rational worldview that is cold enough to be free of neurotic naval gazing in order to capture resources for the nest regardless of niceties. One view for the homestead and one view for the battlefield. This necessity of the nest is most clear with doctors and nurses. One must come into a situation free from emotional anxiety to perform gut wrenching tasks requiring clear rational focus while the other must be there to nurture the patient who must submit themselves to the coldness of the scalpel.

The issue in our times is that the egg carrying nesters who are designed for emotional nurturing and infant care are being socialized into a cold worldview while the utilitarian design of the males whose role in reproduction is the moment of giving seed to the egg are being socialized into the role of nurturing caregiver to children. The males of our species are designed for a brief expulsion of seed without bearing children in womb because biological imperative is to be the independent one for resource gathering for the female. This is the root reason why males are designed for provision and protection. It is because of the freedom from caring children in womb that most frees them for hunt and exploration. The innate hormone flux in the females of our species creates a necessary anxiety of self that compels them to regulate themselves socially to ease that anxiety which makes them more attune to emotional empathy for nurturing.

What happens when nurses are taught to be cold and doctors are taught to be warm? We get emotional surgeons and detached caregivers. We get surgeons afraid to cut into the flesh and who let death overwhelm them into crushing despair while unempathetic nurses spike the anxiety in the patients recovering from surgery. This can be fundamentally seen in the upbringing of modern children who are raised by stay-at-home fathers while their mothers act as providers. The fathers at home cannot match the innate warmth and empathy of what the mother could offer while the mother cannot detach herself from the emotional self-sacrifice of careerism.

Let us now go to the divide.

We have a rise of single women in our times who are aging alone. What does this mean for the world at large? It means that the innate reproductive anxiety of these females will express itself through all their political choices. They will not have the rational worldview and cold masculine frame to balance their own. This means they will try to force their reproductive anxiety in all aspects of their belief systems. The hostility between the sexes will continue to skyrocket as females become unfamiliar with anything outside their singular worldview. An entire generation of females are either being raised without fathers or with fathers who are in the feminine frame of authority. These women have little to no men in their lives who challenge them with a fundamentally different perspective on reality. The collective hive mind of the feminine frame of authority will seek to destroy all challenges to its unifying vision. When women have little to no men in their lives that hold a masculine psychology that they respect, they will be more apt to see all opposing views to their own as a threat to their own emotional hopes for the world.

These egg carrying nesters will seek out the few men who act like roaming roosters to propagate with them and then they will carry great hatred over males because the men they desire do not hang around to protect/provide. So, they vent their complaint over all men even though it is a few males who have sexual access. They will complain about a polygamous system of sexual selection where they cannot secure their needed providers that has only arisen because of how their own careerism has disenfranchised the vast number of males. And so, they will only have experience with a few males who refuse to commit to them which imbitters them to all men as "toxic." This creates a dual state of indignation in a woman's mind as she either sees a male as an irresponsible cad or an undesirable "incel." Women in our times have tremendous hatred for men in general because the few men they truly desire do not want to commit and the majority of men leer at them in sexual desperation. This increases the amount of disrespect that women vent to each other in their insular echo chambers about men in general. And what happens if a female happens to find a man who meets her burden of performance and is willing to commit to her? Her entire social circle will project all their own personal biases on her in jealous rage. The female who can find and secure a masculine male will be viewed as a traitor to the "strong and independent" image of her surrounding peers. Her peer group will project onto the woman's submission as reckless because they see men as either promiscuous dogs or sexless creeps. But more importantly, their friend's submission to a masculine man is a further reminder that their own reproductive anxiety is not being solved. And it is a further reminder of their own desire for submission that conflicts with the independence that has freed them undesired pairings in our selection. Nothing brings more resentment in female social networks than a woman who happily submits to a man's frame. Women will be more than happy to celebrate a female who dominates a male who meets her burden of performance but will see it as a threat to their own power of independence when a woman finds a man who holds power over her.

The more single females we have in our world, the more these female's social circles will celebrate independence from males to not only save face but to reassure the sadness in each other. It is common for women to either complain about their unframed providers, asshole protectors or the repulsive sexless men that surround them. This framework of complaint against men is the ground rule to reassure the majority that are unhappy in love.

When a female is happy in submission with a male, she will be afraid to reveal this dynamic to her friend group because it shines a light on their discontents.

Interrupting

the

orgy

The breakdown of monogamous pair bonding between the sexes is a result of female liberation and this has increased all sexual liberation in its wake. The reason why sexual liberation follows female liberation movements is because sexual openness most benefits women who want freedom from undesirable pairings from monogamy. The root reason is that females want most access to valuable seed from increased promiscuity and faux polygamous arrangements inherent to female sexuality. They are able to secure valuable genetic seed to impregnate them before securing an inferior male provider for the offspring. Of course, females want monogamous relationships with these rare desirable males but will be forced to seek providers for the desirable male's offspring. This allows them to carry the best genetic gift to the next generation of our species. Remember, women sought financial independence in our world because they were priorly forced into monogamy with inferior males who were allowed to continue their genetic legacy because they served a role as needed providers.

All sexual liberation most benefits the hidden agenda in female's nature of securing the best genetic seed from attractive males and their financial independence allows them the liberation to pursue this course. Civilization is an agreement between men just as a system of monogamy is an agreement between men. Monogamy most benefits males who would never have continued their genetic legacy forward in other systems. This is the fundamental reason why women fight for not just financial liberation but also push sexual liberation. The genetic pool is narrowed to a few with newfound access which allows them choice to bear superior offspring and not be biologically saddled with the genetic material from an inferior male. The fertility cult of true male empowerment is in equal distribution of genetic legacy with males that females would not normally choose in a system where they do not need to rely on them for provider-ship.

The starting promiscuity among heterosexual males and females when the sexual revolution happened during mid twentieth century across western civilization was this capturing of few genetic material of desirable males over the majority. Something that could not happen in a religiously monogamous culture where women bore the children of sexually mediocre males. But after the sexual freedom of heterosexuals created a new polygamous reality where few males now have sexual access to majority females, this influenced the feminist support for homosexual males. It may seem weird to a man that a heterosexual female would make it a focal point to fight for sexual liberation among homosexual men but it will make sense to him with the broad scope of sexual selection within perspective. The sexual liberation that women have pushed for has created a vast divide between the sexes. The haves and the have nots. Feminists will spend countless hours talking about financial disparity with the few holding the wealth over the majority but will completely ignore the very basis of our financial system, our sexual selection. Sexual liberation has created a tremendous disparity of sexual access between a few males and the majority. While a few males are oversexed by holding causal harems, a great many males are undersexed and even sexless. Women innately understand this problem unconsciously which compels them to support males having sex with another. Homosexuality among males converts potential sexual threats of virgin males to women into harmless redirections towards each other. The absurdity of why a heterosexual female would make it a singular political issue to fight for the rights of homosexuality among men will begin to make sense. It is the quelling of potential sexual threats into something sexually harmless that women most support. The support for homosexual males by feminists comes from their high sexual anxiety over the surrounding sexual desperation among men. Think about it like this, there are ten men and ten women in a room, two men have all the women interested in them which leaves eight men to themselves. The women will think "I wish the remaining male would take sexual interest in each other, that would calm the anxiety we feel about this unfairness from our nature." This is why we have a rise of males experimenting outside heterosexual norms and a growing rise of virgin males known as "incels."

The sexual revolution represents not just the feminine biological imperative to capture the most desirable genetic material from a few males but also the breakdown the family that was previously based on monogamy. A father with a mother bearing children. This is the great prison that the female liberation movement freed itself from. The genetic chains of monogamous pairings with inferior males. The majority of women had to submit their bodies to men that they had little respect for. The very idea of female submission in families held deep resentment and disgust for women for centuries. Women inherently in genetic greed wanted better seed for their wombs. They would climb and claw over each other to share the few males of their desires. And the remaining males could watch as impotent cucks through digital means or they could have sex with each other.

But what this sexually liberated generation do not realize is that the sexual revolution is not designed to last just like all female power movements. The sexual revolution is chaos. Feminine is chaos. Why? *What has no clear rules become unraveled by the eventuality of its course*. Just as a game where the rules are in constant change based on feelings cannot last, so too will the sexual revolution come to an end. The great divide between the haves and have nots is reaching fever pitch, and the have nots grow restless. This is the same for any system of government or game. When the game fails, people not only stop playing but they want to establish a new game. When unemployment skyrockets and people cannot feed themselves and families is when revolutions happen. This will soon be true of the sexual liberation movement. It is creating too much disparity to support itself. But even the rulebook is becoming more confused and confused as the days continue on. The movement needs new battles to satisfy the young generation and to keep people politically focused which means that the rules need to keep expanding with the new battles. This is why the sexual revolution started first with "free love" between heterosexuals before opening up to homosexuals before opening up to transexuals and so forth. In fact, the letters of LGBT are no longer relevant as it excludes newfound identifies that are being explored. But the infertility cult of feminine frame psychology eventually collapses from its fruitlessness. A new battle is the normalizing of adoption from non-heterosexual parents. This has been happening side by side with the teaching young children of the long list of non-normative sexual behaviors. This will have a massive psychological influence on children pursuing relationships outside the normal monogamous male/female dynamic. And so, we see a rise of feminist parents taking their children to drag shows as a way to open their minds to acceptance while not realizing they are conditioning these same children into fruitless behaviorism which further expands the decrease in population. Even sometimes a feminist mother will allow the child to physically castrate themselves. Once a man understands that all feminist ideology is based on reproductive anxiety, it will open his eyes to the celebration of fruitless sexual behaviorism in our times. It is disbelief in the future and greedy obsession with the moment. All feminist ideology is based on infertility or the refusal to propagate with the majority of males. But the sexless males who are made to watch from afar will not watch a game that they are not allowed to play for much longer.

This is why we will without doubt see a revolt against the sexual liberation movement in coming years. Divorce rates are skyrocketing, marriage rates are collapsing, birth rates are dropping and fatherlessness is increasing. The system is failing because of sexual behaviorism. What this generation will soon realize is that sex has meaning between males and females. That a generation of men were given sexual poverty and genetic death. They were told to watch from the sidelines while women ran free from them. We will see mass shootings spring up from around the world as sexless men see no reason to live. The game has failed them and so they act as anarchists to it. This "incel fear" is what most terrorizes feminists and women in general. They know that their gaslighting with homosexual celebration will not quench the sexual thirst from the rise of sexless males. What this generation forget is that orgies are not meant to last. What this generation forget is that they cannot free one animal without freeing the other. The greedy impulses that are indulged with one animal only inspires the other animal to watch in resentment. All sexual liberations in history leads to violent revolutions. The Weimar Republic led to Nazi Germany. There is always a war on degeneracy when the degeneracy itself starts to dissolve all the existing intuitions. The family is dying slow in western civilization and children are being prey upon as a final supper before the end comes. The animal in this generation's heart is becoming craven in its final pursuit of pleasure. No belief beyond the moment. No belief in tomorrow. Only a belief in the eternal moment and animal impulse. The only concern in this generation is how to keep the orgy going. The only care is how to protect the orgy from interruption. They do not want the feast to end. They do not want to have to admit their selfishness and lack of care for this young generation. Women will never admit that they led this generation of children into reproductive death. And so, they will double down on something they refuse to understand. The responsibility of passing belief onto the next generation. A belief in human life. A belief in tomorrow. A father's belief in his son.

Earned ego and humility

Men start at the bottom in sexual selection and must climb up whereas women start at the top and slide down. A man must fail over and over in sexual selection to figure out a female's behaviors so as to overcome her misleading verbal subterfuge and guarded nature. A man must become while a woman merely needs to be. This inherent need for adaptation in sexual selection creates both an earned ego as well as sense of humility in the males of our species. When a woman fails to capture a man's interest in selection, she will puff up her ego and deny that she needs to learn a lesson. But a man in selection when he is rejected by a female will become inward looking to how he failed to capture her interest. Men must become like salesman in sex while women must present themselves as customer to the advances and strategies of men. This is root reason why men become strategists in worldly affairs and are conditioned into problem solving. We must solve our sexual problem which compels us into this frame of thinking.

The way each sex handles rejection in our selection informs their behaviorism in all things. As men, we must not feel defeated in rejections by women, we must not let it affect our ego but also, we must not view our behaviors as perfect. We are able to separate behavior from love of self. Women inherently see themselves as complete and do not separate their egos from their actions. It is a sense of being versus becoming. It is a privilege of passivity. A woman's emotional protection of ego defense which puffs up her sense of self is what prevents her from the humility necessary for adaptation.

What separates animals from humans? It is our high consciousness. What is that higher consciousness? It is the humility needed to abandon failed strategies. It is the humility needed to break mad loops. We can rise above our own behaviors with a God's Eye and look upon failed repetitions. We can rise above all living things and see the repetitions in their behaviorism. This is what it means to game an animal as a hunter. Man is the ultimate hunter in reality. We know what it means to bait and trap. We know our own weaknesses and the weaknesses of our enemies. This means we must not moralize weakness. This means we cannot lie to protect our ego. Humility is sight to the blind. It is the gateway to higher consciousness. A higher consciousness that separates males from females. It is conditioned humility in the sexual selection of our species. Women create barriers and walls for men to transcend and overcome. Sex is problem solving and man is the fundamental problem, not the woman. Aha. See? Females create problems to overcome. But in reality, females point to the problems that exist in a male's behaviorism. Sex makes us better as not just men but as a species. Women train men to lead, they train men to overcome weak behaviorism, they encourage men to overcome neurotic insanities. How a woman protects her sexuality from men is the greatest act of cheerleading in existence. This is something that a female will never truly understand. The difficulty she places on males in sexual selection creates the needed humility for higher consciousness and therefore supremacy. There is no bigger motivator in our existence then the primal urge of passing our legacy down through reproduction before we die. Procreate and die. This is the eternal truth of all living organisms in reality. This is the core wisdom that motivates all our behavior and the beating heart behind the complexities of modern civilization.

This takes us to the rationale that is necessary for higher order. To make sense of reality, reality must first be defined. Even a blind man in darkness must organize his environment and how his other senses align with it to help him overcome it. The high amount of failure and rejection that a male experiences in sexual selection helps him to calibrate the definitions of his mistakes so as to form a new strategy. The human female is symbolic of chaos because female consciousness is all encompassing in a state of being. This can be likened to water on a flat surface that spreads out whereas male consciousness is based on becoming or the defining boundaries that give meaning to the meaningless. The reason why males are rational or better yet, have the capacity for greater rationality than females is because of two fundamental elements. The male sex organ is a clear definition in objectivity that the male must navigate as a tool in his environment with playfulness that influences how he perceives novel configurations around him. This is the biological start to our psychology. The psychological reason that is built atop is the start to how a man is informed by the burden of performance that females place upon him in our sexual selection. This places on a man a fundamental problem he must solve to succeed in his own biological necessity. And this is not to say that all males are more rational than all females but males have the capacity for much greater rationality than females by design of not just in body but also conditioning from sexual strategy.

The vast expectations that females place on males in our selection are preparations for fatherhood and leadership in general. A major reason why wise men in the past would prepare young boys as "future leaders" was not only to give them a running head start in sexual selection but also to align them to the need for strong leadership in the world.

Let us now focus on females in our selection. A woman presents herself in passivity as a chooser to a man's advances. She sits on her eggs in judgment in the conscious and unconscious judging of the male's behaviorism for ultimate benefit in reproduction. This creates a large ego in females as they start with their ultimate value in fertility that is represented by youthful beauty which draws male attention. They fall into haughty arrogance as powerful men give them sexual attention early in their life cycle and they choose their own suitors. This puffery that is inherent to females in sex is a façade to the innate uncertainty of self that women carry from sex organ blindness and irrational sense self from the duality of their hormone flux. A woman holds great uncertainty about herself and her own body which she realizes is her own burden of performance, but that inherent low self-esteem is externally puffed up by the male gaze itself when she is in the bloom of her fertility. This is the root reason why a female cannot emotionally handle rejection in our selection which prevents her from the ultimate humility that creates a power of adaptation. When a female is sexually rejected, her puffed up sense of self is deflated which leaves her in a void of self-loathing. And so rather than give meaning to the external world that rejects her, she gives further meaning to her not having to conform to the will of others by gaslighting herself to hold higher esteem as a way to inflate the previous puffery. This why man is a learning animal and why a woman stays stagnant in her personality from youth to old age. Her self does not need to adjust itself to the surrounding world, but rather she protects her ego by expecting the world to bend itself to her. But this is not true in an absolute sense but rather mostly true. Absoluteness rarely exists leaving us clearly defined degrees of difference. The one small way a woman learns in sexual selection is how she mitigates her losses through increased sexual defenses and higher expectations of the burden of performances of males. We see this when a woman ages. *She will double her ego when she loses half her eggs*. This is why a woman at thirty will more difficult than a woman at twenty. The rejections and romantic failures that she experienced prior has increased her ego by the gaslighting puffery. And this works to a degree but only on men who are ignorant of design or who have low self-esteem. They will believe the self-enforced inflation of currency that women place on their value because they are grateful for the opportunity, even if late.

The difference between a male and female in sexual selection can be likened to an adventurer who ventures into a cave that holds treasure. Before a man enters a cave, he must lower his head for entrance. This is an example of what humility means. It means we must realize that the world will not expect our shape as it currently is and that we must bend ourselves to fit into the world. To lack humility is to either hit the head on the cave entrance in self-harm over and over in unlearning repetitions which is the definition of madness or to choose to walk away from the cave because it requires us to change ourselves to enter. This is how a man needs to think about our sexual selection and how that would inform our psychology. When a female approaches the cave of sexual selection, if she hits her head, she will most times walk away telling herself that "there are plenty of other caves that would take me the way she I am," and, "that cave probably does not even hold treasure," and, "if the cave holds treasure, I do not even want it" and so forth. This is all ego defense from not just failure but the refusal of humility. And this is the root reason why the males of our species have the capacity for greatness in ambition and problem solving.

Blinding the male gaze

The fall of monogamy was followed by the rise of virgin men. Men who would have normally been paired off with women in their community are now left at a distance with only their eyes to satisfy them. When the divide between males and females becomes vast only the male gaze remains. Eyes full of sexual thirst and desperation. Eyes that possess desire and want. Eyes that act as precursor to possible advances and touch. A touch that sends horror into a female's body. She does not want to carry desperate seed. She does not want this generation of sexless men seeing her. This is why pornography is supported by feminists and why they celebrate it. Females who would normally cohabit with undesirable males that provide resource to them and bear their children can now extract resources from a distance. They no longer have to bear their children and they do not have to give up their resources. We see a rise of digital prostitution in our times as females sell their bodies to the desperate male gaze. But females unconsciously know that a man's arousal is based through his eye.

The free proliferation of pornography is a beggar's banquet that satisfy the collapse of our sexual selection. Virgin males masturbate in self-castration as the images flood their eyes and kill their own erotic imagination. Porn blinds the male gaze. It not only allows the vast majority of men to satisfy their animal heat but also it pacifies them into impotent submission. They become like eunuch voyeurs to the world that surrounds them and fall into an erotization of their own cuckoldry. Digital prostitution gives a man the fantasy of kings with only peasant legacies. Females extract resources from male providers at a safe distance with no threat of impregnation. We live in an age where men can no longer get erections because they have desensitized their own sense of arousal. *Feminists encourage homosexuality and pornography because it solves the sexless male problem*. They either want men to redirect their thirsty gaze to each other or blind themselves with porn. This generation of men walk the earth in castrated downward glances. They have become sexually harmless and this reassures the majority of female's reproductive anxiety. What a man must realize is that all sexual liberation is in the feminine frame of authority. This is why all female empowerment movements are followed by sexual liberation movements. Women unconsciously know that monogamous family arrangements are destroyed by sexual freedom which liberates them from the reproductive burden of our male population.

A man's arousal is based on his erotic imagination and his willpower over his own sex anxiety. Men become aroused not just by their eyes but in their fantasy of potential touch. It is the distance that closes between gaze and touch that fuels male arousal. It is not just "what would that women look like undressed but also how would she feel in my hands?" A two-part story of sexual obsession. What do we find in male dominant societies? Women are encouraged in clothed modesty and pornography is outlawed. That is true male empowerment. Why? Because female modesty not only quiets a woman's sexual advertising but also strengthens the male population's erotic imaginations. Remember, the feminine frame is the cult of infertility while masculine frame is the cult of fertility. The more power women get in this world, the more they will fear the impregnation from less powerful men. A woman is designed for submission and a man's more powerful frame over her calms her reproductive anxieties. Birth rates collapse from female empowerment for this very reason. All feminist political action is based on sex anxiety. How to solve the unwanted male gaze and how to redirect male sexual desire away from them is their key concern. When females dress in modesty and when sex remains a mystery in male's minds causes them to remain sexually strong in virality. Young men must protect their eyes against sexual imagery. They must protect themselves from a world that wants them blind. View all pornography as cock poison. View it is as slave bread meant to keep a man satisfied in his imprisonment.

After I experienced sexual disloyalty from my wife, I had tremendous sex anxiety. I fell into pornography addiction and began erotizing my own cuckoldry. The anxiety that I held made me want to abuse myself. This is the fundamental truth of porn use among men. It is a form of self-abuse. What a man is doing when he is a frequent masturbator and porn viewer is castrating himself. The more a man indulges himself in watching other men have sex with women, the more he is conditioning himself into passive cuckold acceptance over his reality. He is unconsciously trying to destroy his own sex organ in madness. The eye becomes blind and the erection becomes weak. This is what happens with porn addiction. It is a destroying of the body and mind for weak willed pleasures. A pleasure that is given only with a devil's bargain. Not only does the mind blind his own eye but he castrates himself of sexual power. This generation of men have become impotent from that devil's delight. They have traded a life of sexual fruitfulness for fruitless insanity. This is the root reason behind our minds when we recognize our own madness. We know we must not procreate and therefore we castrate ourselves of that potential.

Men who have battled madness for thousands of years have also castrated themselves to prevent that madness from spreading to the next generation. The rise of men in their feminine frame who were raised fatherless has made them become imitators of female neurotic behaviorism and reproductive fear. They castrate themselves with pornography as a way to not only placate the animal heat that exists within them but also to destroy their own capacity to spread their seed.

What can a man do when he is battling porn addiction? He must first recognize it as a poison that rots his own sex organ. He must recognize that he is acting not only in weak willed indulgence but also weakening his own erections. Once a man begins to view erotic display as causing sexual blindness, he will begin to protect his eye from what is worthless. He will then notice his sexual power returning. There is hope in repair. The body is a miracle in fixing itself. But we must stop poisoning it so that he can begin to heal. While I do not recommend masturbating to orgasm, I do recommend men who are battling erectile dysfunction to achieve erection based on erotic imagination alone. This helps them to see that they can will the power needed for sex with their mind alone. But do not orgasm. Stay away the darkness of this world that blinds and push away these peasant pleasures.

Seeing in the dark

This generation of men who were made blind by the over stimulation of their eyes must find another way. What can a man do when his own arousal is limited by the collapse of his erotic imagination and the desensitation of his eye? He must venture into the dark. He must listen to the wisdom of female arousal. As men, we look upon the world in our male gaze to capture sexual interest. We learn to overly rely on the eye for our erotic stimulation. If a man is losing his erection in the middle of the sex act, he needs to find a new way to hold his own excitement. A lot of men in our times have been sexually blinded on purpose to pacify them into a state of harmlessness. The greatest fear that a woman holds is to be raped by an inferior and desperate male. The widespread propagation of free pornography is a tool to blind the male gaze so as to create an epidemic of males who could not pose a risk of rape to females. They have been neutered not by physical force but by digital allures. They walk the earth blind in search of erotic meaning. Our generation more than any other generation have been destroyed and disempowered on purpose.

The vast majority of males that are no longer in monogamous arrangements and who no longer have the dignity of a family are viewed as a liability to the feminine imperative. They exist like worker drones who are fed stoic teachings to make them strong in their own invisibility. They are encouraged to be good soldiers standing in the dark of their own despair. These suffering men no longer have sexual virility and power to transform the world. Their erections have softened and their imaginations have been torn from their skulls. Only cartoon vulgarities can stimulate this infantilized age of men. They cling to their perversions that arouse a small pulse of blood into their sex organs only to desensitize them further into a dead state.

We no longer realize that only by fasting can we achieve hunger. We no longer realize that only by modesty can we rebuild the eye. A beautiful women's body hidden in delicate cloth and yet burning bright in our minds. Close your eyes when in the middle of sexual heat. Close your eyes and do not focus on the female body. Do not focus on the hand that touches. Focus on the single erogenous zone that we carry. One singular objective point in the wet acceptance and embrace of a woman's body. She accepts us and we must have faith to let go of our eyes. Only touch and feel. We are with her in the dark. Her fingers close our eye lids. There is only the touch of skin and what possibilities exist in our minds. This is the natural state of a female who understands her own pleasure. Eyes closed. No light in the darkness. Total surrender to the innate darkness of female psychology. Women have never relied on their eyes for sexual arousal and a man can learn from this when his own eyes fail. This is a way to rebuild the tower of stimulation that we build in our mind. Think. Why does a man become aroused by his eye? The eye is merely a trigger to the erotic imagination. It is a trigger to possibilities of touch and ownership by hand. It is a trigger to the arousal of our penetration. The eye is only a start, it is not the end. When a man relies too much on his eye or when his eye has been burned out by too much pornography it is not the eye itself that died but the erotic imagination in his mind that has diminished. Pornography is the death of imagination. It is vulgarities laid bare in the spotlight of what is and not what can be. It destroys the capacity for erotic planning as the vulgar images cuts a preplanned plot that removed the mental struggle that creates conflict needed for stimulation. Conflict is good. Conflict is great. Conflict in the mystery of sex is what creates the greatest arousal. Porn kills our minds. It kills our arousal. Porn is cock poison. But do not give up hope in yourself. Do not let the sex anxiety increase a fear of performance. You can overcome this. But you must have faith in the darkness of delight. Protect the eye. Protect the eye from this world that seeks to blind you. But just as importantly, do not fear letting go of the eye and surrendering yourself to touch.

A denial of will

It has become common for females to defend homosexual males not just because they are defending their incel fear but also because it represents freedom from reproductive imperative. They cheerlead males of our species who lead the way to biological oblivion. True female liberation based on their reproductive anxiety is to be free from giving birth. And the homosexual male represents a joyous celebration of the reproductive dead end. Women are designed to follow male leadership and homosexual males represent a happy march to end times. No belief in continuing the genetic legacy, only a celebration in the pleasure of today over the responsibility of tomorrow. The root reason for females obsessing over homosexual males is one of utter selfishness to their own reproductive anxiety. This is why they will make a showy display of defending homosexual males at all costs because it is a covering to the truth within themselves that they refuse to see. But their fundamental logic is flawed. How? Because they ignore the genetic proclivities in heterosexual males. A female will say a homosexual male is "born this way" while denying that heterosexual males who are promiscuous are "born this way." They will say "even if promiscuity is inherent to all males (the heterosexual males of their interest), we are not animals, we can rise above our behaviorism and design. *We have free will.*" They place this burden of free will and animal denial not on homosexual males but only on heterosexual males.

What is the truth of our animal design?

A male's inherent nature is to spread his seed with as many females as he can before he dies. This is why a man will have deep urges into promiscuous behavior even if he is in a relationship with a female. He falls easily into sexualizing females with his male gaze because the hidden code within is telling him to keep spreading his seed. Prior to civilization, this nature was used to keep our species alive. Life was brutally cut short either from disease or wildlife or Nephilim savagery. If a man could impregnate a female, there was a long list of reasons that the child would not survive to adulthood. The conception could fail, the pregnancy could fail or the infant could die within the first few years of life. It was truly a miracle when a child survived long enough to die tragically by middle age. This was the reality of the brutality of human existence before modern civilization. And this is a reason why men are programmed to spread their seed far and wide. Think about males and females not just like seed and egg but rather as seed upon soil. A farmer knows that growing a bountiful harvest requires a cornucopia of good elements all working along with each other. Good soil, good seed, good weather and lots of sunshine. The same for our human race. Why would the majority of females be morally accepting of homosexual promiscuity but not heterosexual promiscuity? Is not born this way also *born this way*? The difference is one of responsibility to the child that is shared between the male and female. Women expect more from heterosexual men because it the family arrangement that is a shared responsibility and women want to be reassured that men will commit to that responsibility. This is why women are attracted to protectors/providers in our species. They place a high burden of performance on heterosexual men because they expect these men to lead them away from reproductive anxiety and to care for them while they are incapacitated with child.

Remember, a woman's reasoning is emotionally influenced but the emotionalism itself hides the most selfish reasons in their sexual selection. This is why a female will defend the sexual behaviorism of all the males except the heterosexual ones. She destroys her own logic by holding fast to her own selfish imperative. If a female said "homosexual males are born this way, leave them alone and heterosexual males are born promiscuous too" would make her logic at least line up without conflict. But no. She expects heterosexual males to summon this thing we call "free will" to rise above their own animal nature and to serve her own animal needs. Our human capacity to use our free will to control our animal proclivities is how we can order ourselves enough for civilization. Otherwise, there is only sex and violence. The surrender to the animal is to shrug accountability for the human. And if we want to continue believing that we are above animal violence then we need to admit that we can also rise above the chaos of our sexual behaviorism. We either can control ourselves or we cannot. To surrender the consciousness into one of being over becoming is the feminine frame of authority. A reason why "live for the day" indulgences snowball in a civilization in its death throes. Everyone wants have their pleasure but nobody wants to live with the consequences. The reason why a human is different from animals is that we can break loops that spiral us into decay and death. Something is wrong. Something must be corrected. There is a way forward that is different from previous attempts. This is how we as a species survive and how we as men rise above ourselves. We must become means not only having free will but also the capacity to use that will as a precious gift. A gift of change. A gift of sanity. A gift in knowing our missteps.

Women

cannot

bear

hiding

their

inner

shadows

A woman relies emotionally on external validation to stabilize her feelings of uncertainty. It is no coincidence that females want heterosexual men to not express themselves while at the same time celebrating homosexuality. Think about it like this. A woman has to endure emotional vulnerability each month with her down cycle. Her hormones flux which creates an uncertain feeling in her consciousness. This monthly battle creates a whirlpool of uneasiness that is relieved by her expression to friends. They innately see expression as necessary for their sanity. *And it is*. But what they falsely assume is that what is good for women would be good for men. That is arrogance and ignorance. During this monthly cycle they depend on group reassurance while feeling vulnerable to group excommunication. In ancient times, if a woman was excommunicated from her collective, she would be overwhelmed with feelings of suicide because she knew that without the group she would die in isolation.

A woman aligns herself with the collective for her own survival both physically and emotionally. To be outside the group is a feeling of death. In a feminized environment women will be champions for people who are on the outside of a group. This can be a beautiful thing as outsiders are not necessarily villains but are merely misunderstood. And if a person who is an outsider is accepted into a group but is prevented from expressing their feelings, it pains a woman's deep sense of empathy. *To hold back expression is to be deprived of the emotional validation necessary for being a woman.* That is why women encourage men to express themselves because they are thinking through the uneasy and vulnerable lens of their own biology. This biology informs their psychology which creates an *emotional worldview.* They depend on collective reassurance not only for emotional validation but for their innate ancestral memory of needing fellow women to help them with child rearing when their men were at hunt or war.

This sets the frame for understanding why women encourage men to express themselves. They view reality through the lens of "isolation from group is misery and death" When they say, "just be yourself" to men, it is because they want to "just be themselves" too. Women expand indulgent neuroticisms because they rely on emotional comfort to ease their existential anxiety and fear. That is why there is a simultaneous celebration of fatness and homosexuality with women. It goes with the "just be yourself" mindset while accepting people who feel shamed from the group. Feminists worship at the altar of "born this way" for sexuality and fatness because it frees the person from feeling anxiety over the responsibility of changing themselves. It is how they solve problems through their emotional lens while allowing themselves and others to be free from accountability. They will never say "maybe your sexuality is a psychological issue" Or "maybe your overeating is a psychological issue with dealing with stress." They will never say these sentences because it requires the person to work towards changing themselves which goes against the rule of "just be yourself." And expecting a person to change themselves for self-betterment is overwhelming to feminized beings who rely on neurotic comforts to ease their anxiety. In a way, I myself can understand this with my OCD. One of my brothers once said: "Why is your hands bleeding?" (my hands were dry and cracked) This made me feel bad which caused me to go into defense over my behavior. "I have obsessive compulsive disorder", I said in my own defense. "Why don't you try not to wash your hands so much?" He replied

His blunt and masculine speech drove me mad at the time. In my mind I would think: *He is ignorant and simple*. I felt overwhelmed by his bluntness at the time as if he were bullying me needlessly. In retrospect he was correct while being simple. He didn't give me specific advice on how to overcome my neuroticism (desensitization therapy), but his willingness to speak out against my psychological issue is the key difference between men and women. No women around me at the time were telling me that I could overcome my disorder. They would just tip toe in their speech to not hurt my feelings and ignore it altogether.

With the rise of fatherlessness and with men being encouraged to be like women we are seeing a mass rise in mental illness because everyone is controlled by sensitivity. We need less celebration of neuroticism and more speech bringing attention to disorders. Instead of celebrating a woman who overeats, her neurotic behavior should be addressed. Instead of blindly accepting all forms of sexuality as empowerment, we need to start helping people get psychological treatment. When we hear a person speaking of having sex with their couch, we should bring attention to the oddness and not celebrate it before a growing generation of children. It is as if we are grooming children to be mad because our forgotten generation lacks the social bravery needed to stand up for sanity.

We need to disconnect the false connection of the civil rights movement from sexual neuroticism. A person's obsessive-compulsive disorder should not be compared to a person's struggle based on their skin color. Sexuality is a mixture of biology AND psychology. A person's skin color is just biology. This is a false equivalence and must stop. This false connection is increasing mental illness from its false view of empowerment which is creating a massive decline in the consciousness of our world. We are told by feminists that "love is love" when a person has a certain sexual disorder. There is not a more meaningless set of words than "love is love." It is used to gaslight a confused generation to shut off their rationality and just accept the madness. How would a feminist even define a sexual disorder, or do they not exist in a feminist utopia?

There are a lot of men who allow madness to rise because they weakly follow the mindset of "not for me to judge" along with a mindset of "live and let live." Or the incredibly limp and impotent "It's all good."

These sayings begin to get complicated when there are political campaigns to indoctrinate children with sexual neuroticism. We know why women would allow madness to rise but is there a few globalists elite manipulating the feminist agenda? *Do they want to groom children for sexual confusion to lower birth rates in order to save the climate*? Do they want to sexually groom children before a future revelation that would show power figures of the world having abused children? Would that cause them to work overtime to normalize sexuality and children? Is this the endpoint of moral relativism and postmodern thought? That all sexuality is a construct and therefore all sexual demonization is a construct to be formed and controlled by propagandists? These are higher level thoughts that exist above feminists, but some may be true. We will have to wait and see.

The thing to remember is that feminists equate sexuality with empowerment and will keep working towards empowering all sexual expressions until masculine men stop them. They view "furniture sexuality" the same as the black civil rights movement because they are being led along by their emotion and do not realize the rules they are creating. (or total lack of rules to their mission.) It is merely about adding more colors to the rainbow and getting more people to join them in the madness parades.

A woman is two things at once

The female of our species holds great uncertainty over her sense of self. The lack of objective meaning from her genitalia out of sight, and her duality from her hormone flux, causes her to hold doubt over an objective view of herself. She sees herself as nothing and everything. A reason why a woman holds puffed up self-esteem that can be easily deflated. She is both triumphant and vulnerable in her own menstrual cycle. One half of the month she is riding high while the other half she is low. This up and down rhythm to a female's biology creates an up and down conditioning to her psychology. This doubt of self can be easily seen as young girls will hold fascination over boys before boys hold fascination over girls. Young girls will find boys out to watch as the boys play at their own objective meanings. They either identify away from or with the boys at play.

The uncertain nature of a female makes her reactionary to the certain nature of a male. She either aligns herself to the inherent qualities of him or aligns herself in how to be a compliment to his nature. The male is the stable guiding identifier in female psychology. Remember, we can only make sense of madness when we give it a method and we can only make sense of chaos when we order it in our minds. Just like all problem solving, we must first think about the unchanging or common aspects to a problem as a way to frame the unknowns that surround it. This is a grounding affect that allows us to be able to have a starting position to push off from as to seek an answer. When something is "pure chaos", that means there is not a repeatable pattern to discern which means that there is not a way to ground ourselves enough to give the chaos meaning. A female is chaos from not only the blind meaning of her genitalia but also from the flux of the hormone that rules her mind. This keeps her in a state of confusion over her own identity which informs her own sexual confusion. The most basic aspect to the meaning of our identity of being a human being is to recognize that we are born to reproduce before death. Reread that. That is the fundamental programming of all living things and that is the foundation of our own psychology.

Having an objective awareness of where we stand in a species based on which sex, we are will either give us certainty or uncertainty. The male has objective focus on his sex organ while the female has subjective awareness of her own organ. A male understands what his organ looks like with his eye and he understands that it holds unique singular pleasure in its purpose. The female is visually blind to her organ which makes her view her own sexuality as subjective in meaning as her pleasure becomes plural from the imaginative diffusion across her body. While a male knows with a certainty where his pleasure lies, a female is in doubt over where her true pleasure exists. A touch on her elbow, a touch on her hair, a touch on her lower back or touch on her leg can send dispersed pulsations of pleasure that electrify her entire body. When something becomes everything, it becomes nothing. The single erogenous zone of a female makes her more sexually open to possibility of excitement which informs her own subjective view of her sexuality. The female body is passive in knowing and relies on guidance for understanding. It is the male eye that excites the female imagination and it is the male hand that directs the female body into new pleasure. The open erogenous zone that covers a female makes her sensitive in arousal. This "openness" in sexual feeling makes her open to the possibilities of novel stimulations. A female will experiment with other females as a way to explore new feelings. She will be curious about "how it feels." This innate confusion over sense of self paired with the entire self being an erogenous zone creates inherent curiosity towards open sexual expression. When a male is expressing sexual openness (sexual confusion) in homosexuality, a female will feel reassured over her own confusion. What a man must realize about females is that they want to be reassured that they are navigating reality with sanity and they use males as guideposts in that calibration. This is a reason why a young daughter tests her father with her own behaviorism. She will explore meaning through his reaction to her so-called rebellious actions. It could be a piercing, a tattoo, dyed hair or coming out as a sexual novelty. The daughter will think "If I am acting in self-harm, it is my father's responsibility to let me know. He needs to tell me whether or not I am acting mad." She will place the burden of sanity on the external validation of her father and will configure herself to his eye.

A father's love can only be discerned late in life when a disciplined view of reality can be understood as sane after trials and errors. This generation either have fathers who act like mothers or no father at all. They will say "I love you the way you are" to their daughters who want to be told they are acting crazy. A female knows that her father holds a special place as a disagreeable figure who has her best interests in heart. If she comes up to her father with something that is daring-to-be-crazy to herself, she will ultimately feel unloved by his continued acceptance over that testing. It takes little thought to blindly accept others behaviorism. "Good, good, good" this generation hear from their parents who do not act as disagreeable guides over their acts of madness. They are cheerleading them off the cliffs of insanity because they are afraid to be hated for a moment. What men need to realize about female nature is that women expect men to calm their crazy feelings not from blind acceptance but from disagreeable truth. But when a generation of males are in imitation to the innate sexual confusion of our female species, females will double down in their psychological testing because they are calibrated from the surrounding males. This is why sexual confusion does not just spread in a feminized world, it snowballs as females continue testing the male environment with new ways to validate their own sanity. They are saying "Am I mad?" and only getting applause from a male audience. And this creates a new normal that compels a new performance of "Am

I mad?" which further degrades the meaning of sanity.

Women are designed to test male sanity and male authority by pushing established boundaries. But that feedback also informs their own behavior as they calibrate themselves to the external acceptance of how they behave. Remember, a young girl will test her father's permissiveness over self-harming behavior to emotionally reassure herself of her own sanity. Once the initial test is accepted as normal, it will compel her into more extreme testing. This is why a daughter will start with multiple piercings before moving to unnatural dyed hair to tattoos to other ways to signal for help over her own anxiety disorders. We are seeing a continued push into more bizarre sexual expression in our times because the previous expression was deemed normal in acceptance. The sexual revolution has no end. It is a runaway train that will consume everything in its path. A female is sexually without border in meaning and only gets meaning from the objective viewpoint of a male. This is why sexual behaviorism is becoming more and more desperate in madness. If homosexuality is good then why is transsexuality bad? If transsexuality is good then why is the new thing bad? See? It is a game without rules and games without rules do not last long. The logic is corrupt at the core and this means that a collapse of the game itself is coming soon.

A woman pushes a man's boundaries as a way to reassure her own openness. Her innate anxiety is calmed not by the soft acceptance of her testing but in the rising above her tests. From above we can view female behavior and our own behavior. We can see how it forms together as ONE species. The male gaze combined with our touch narrows a female's mind from the spread-out mystery of her form to the singular objective of our hand. Men define borders and protect borders. It is our responsibility to act as an external boundary to feminine openness. A dam acts as a barrier between chaos and order just as men act as protectors of sanity. This is why our forefathers only viewed heterosexuality as moral (sane.) Because once the logic is broken by rebelling from biological imperative of reproduction, a spiral of acceptance begins to form. Games rely on logical rule structures just as sex relies on logical rule structures. There is only order or chaos. There is only heterosexuality or madness. To accept anything else is to be irrational in the rules that bind us as a species together. To pick and choose based on emotionalism is to fall prey to flawed logic that will once again create a game design. *Women are meant not to guard rule systems but rather to undermine them.* This is why only males carry traditionalism down through thousands of years. It is the humility we understand through our own sexual selection that makes us bow to ancient wisdoms. It is the ego of the female who thinks she can remake reality in her own image. She is without reverence to history and breaks rule systems. Only masculine men carry heterosexuality down from generation to generation. Heterosexuality is not just a biological imperative but also a male tradition that aligns with biological imperative. That very boundary with its clear definition offends women because it offends their innate open sexuality. And so, they will test us in our times just as they have always tested that rule in all times.

Women want to be held

All sex is about reproduction regardless if that is the conscious intent or not. Once a man understands the animal, he will understand its heat. The difficulty that a female experiences when bearing a child influences her entire sexual selection. For countless millennia, women had to depend on males as protectors and providers while they were incapacitated with child in womb. This is the root reason why a female wants security from a male in sex. The man must reassure her sex anxiety so that she feels safe to accept him as her leader and feels safe enough to surrender not just her body in the sex act but also in pregnancy. A female is seeking a man who can make her feel whole, who makes her feel secure in his possession.

The sex act for a female is a vulnerable act of submission to a man's will. This is the fundamental reason why women consciously and unconsciously look for leader/follower dynamic in sexual selection. The leader's frame holds the follower in possession which creates a craving for belonging in his reality. Females want to be overwhelmed by the presence of male sexuality enough to let go of their own sense of self for total possession. They surf on the pleasure of the male in sex. But remember, this all has deep biological meaning. Women seek strong men in our world because male strength allows them to be shielded enough for a state of vulnerability which is not only the pleasure of the sex act but also the burden of pregnancy. When a female gets supreme pleasure from being dominated by a man in sex, she is getting a high reassurance that the male can handle reality for them both while she focuses her attention away from the world and to her own transforming body. To possess something is to own something and to create a sense of belonging in those caught in possession.

The core element in a female's heart of desire is getting positive attention over her identity. She depends on external validation from peers to regulate her emotionalism which creates a deep longing for belonging. This conditioned craving for belonging from social need translates into that same craving in the sex act. When a woman feels a deep sense of belonging in sex, she feels safe enough to let go because she is in the hands of another. There is a trust building exercise where someone "let's go" and falls into the arms of another that perfectly shows female sexuality. A woman must feel trust to feel safe to let go of herself for total possession in sex to achieve ultimate pleasure. Remember, the greatest barrier to female pleasure in sex is the fear of loss of control. Women are naturally guarded sexually to protect themselves from the threat of impregnation from the horde of genetically inferior men. This high level of guarding of sexual access carries with a woman into sex. She must feel safe enough in a man's hands (or possession) to let go of her guarded state. Once a man leads the sex act with low sex anxiety, confidence and dominance, it reassures the woman that she can fall into the passivity of submission needed for her to let go. It is as if she is floating on water in a man's hands. She is in the man's hands and feels owned by him. This does not make her feel bad but rather makes her feel secure in a sense of belonging. *The more the man acts if he already owns her, the more she falls into her sense of belonging and let's go of her guarded nature.* A major reason why "strong and independent" feminists have sexual dysfunction is because they refused to be possessed by anyone but themselves which hurts them in the bedroom. The way they get around this is through elaborate nerdy rituals of BDSM where they intellectualize their own submission as a way to keep hold of some possession of power. But the fragments of possession they cling to close the gates of their own sexual surrenders. This is why a feminist who rules her roost over her weak male will find it difficult when she asks to be dominated by the male in sex. Her direction of the dominance itself keeps in her possession of herself and therefore there is no true surrender of power. The man is in her hands for control which means he belongs to her, not her to him. Women look for rebellious bad boys in sexual selection because these men are in their own frame of authority and cannot be easily controlled. This is why a man who disobeys a woman's direction in the sex act will spike her arousal. He does not belong to her, she belongs to him. He owns her, she does not own him. She is in his hands, he is not in her hands.

When a male takes lead in sex and does not fear his own pleasure, it acts as a deep reassurance of the strength of his frame over the female which allows her to *fall into her pleasure.* A woman falls into sexual pleasure just as she falls in love. It is all an act of surrender to the moment and an act of surrender to a stronger will. When we surrender to our own weakness, we feel a self-loathing. Then why would a woman want to surrender herself to a man whom she looks down upon? The man must be above her in authority and he must not be weak to her control. He must have a mind of his own and this allows her to leave her own mind to join him. See? *The act of possession is an act of ownership which requires the object of possession to surrender themselves into the will of the controller*. To be possessed means to let go and to fall into the hands of another. To accept their will as stronger and worth joining. When a female experiences true sexual pleasure, she feels the complete surrender of herself to a void of warmth spreading across her whole body. To float on the water of her mystery in the hands of her man. He holds her in the wet acceptance of her body and she no longer sees a world of threats to guard against. All her walls fall and she joins the man's kingdom. Love is war. And a female's surrender is her own greatest victory. Carried away in the arms of her captors and carried away by the currents of touch that hold her in its watery touch. An ego death that allows a breakthrough into transcendence. Snap out of herself. Snap out of her desperate clinging to her own authority. Freedom from walls. Freedom from the tight clutching of guarded sexuality. She can finally let go and be liberated from herself. She can be free from the lie of "strong and independent woman" and fall into the bliss of total submission for a brief moment. And there she will find warm belonging. A belonging that she has been seeking her whole life. Validated completely in body and mind by the male gaze that holds her in passion. She is consumed and disengages herself into hands of her masculine leader. At that moment they both become one flesh. The male lets go for one brief moment as he enters the female. Two minds blink out of existence for a moment as seed meets egg.

How women control

A woman must rely on emotional manipulation to control men. Women use shame and guilt tactics as a means of control among each other and they will attempt to use these same tactics against men in romance. A woman's emotions are the most precious thing to her and they mean everything to her. But also, they are stupid and meaningless things to her as well. Women are inherently in doubt of their own emotional reasoning. But they learn from a young age that emotional display can control people and that guilting is another way to control others. This is why a female will learn to weaponize her tears as a way to get pity from others as a way to make them concede to her will. Emotion is a weapon that is sharpest in a woman's hand. She knows that her own emotional vulnerability can influence others into submission and that the emotional sensitivity in others can be manipulated. Our human race is either ruled by heart, mind, sex organ or by force. We can appeal to the capacity for reason, the capacity for emotion, the appeal of animal desire or force our will on others through violence. Women's two ultimate strategies for control is by either appealing to a man's heart or to his desire for sex.

A woman is most aroused by a man who cannot be controlled. This means that a man must rise above emotional control and sexual control. The man who cannot be controlled by a woman will gain her respect and respect leads to sex. When a man learns to not moralize emotion and to control weak willed sexual impulses will allow him to break free from the feminine frame of authority.

What a man must realize is that emotion hold no morality but it is only by our actions that we are judged, not by our feelings. To feel something is only a spark in the fire of human behaviorism, and to celebrate the spark is to be denied the full capacity of the fire of our potential. In a relationship, a female will use guilt and shame tactics on her man as a way to control him. How are men controlled by emotion? They either apologize in submission to the high emotion that their women display (weaponized crying) or they surrender their authority from a *feeling* of shame. Why would a man hold shame? A female could play upon a man's weak sense of self by making him doubt his own manhood or even his ability as a father. This generation of men more than any other are battling feelings of self-loathing over their male sex. They feel that they were born into a demonic sex that has been the only sex that has committed cruelties in history. Remember, modern feminists tear down men as a way to rise to power. They are more power mad than men. But they cannot compete with men at our own level because men are made superior by the burden of performance that is placed on us. Women rise only when men kneel. This is true in a relationship and this is true across the entire power structures in the world. Female empowerment is dependent on male disempowerment. This is why modern men are made to feel guilty because that guilt is used as a way to make them submit without a fight. A woman does not battle like a man with sword and shield. Her strategy is to get men to drop their sword and shield without a fight. How many guilt systems do modern day feminists push on each other and men? Class guilt, race guilt, sex guilt (heterosexual male) and lots of guilt of ancestor behaviors. Feminists want men to bear the consequences of their ancestors while shrugging accountability for themselves. Why should I, who was abandoned by my father, bear his sins? This is why I have always been free from generational guilt. I have recognized the devious nature of guilt systems that are used to make stronger opponents surrender without a fight.

It is all mind games. It is all a manipulation for gained power. There is a common saying that goes "The greatest trick the devil ever pulled in is in convincing the world he does not exist." This is also true of women and power. The greatest trick that a woman pulls on a man is convincing him that she does not seek power over him while she secures that power. Feminists will spend their entire lives fighting for power while demonizing men as power mad. The sooner a man realizes that there is an inherent conflict of interest between the sexes and it is based on power, the sooner he will be able to fight for his own power. Our sexes are in conflict in our species because that conflict makes us better as a species. Conflict means that we must be sharp and strong. When men are gaslit into easy surrender with their women, these women earned that power over their men and they know it. The strongest mind in a relationship should rule it. A major problem in our times is that men are weak minded and easy to mind control. This is why I write books. Because men are being led into slavery to the feminine frame of authority and women cannot even lead themselves properly. It is the blind leading the blind to destruction. This is my own selfish reason for helping men. We need strong men with independent minds to lead women away from their own chaos. Our world is falling apart not because of female strength but because of male weakness. Men have no fight in them. They too easily surrender to emotion and sexual desperation. And so, they are controlled by their women's will to power. There is a scripture in the Bible at Jeremiah 17:9 that says "The heart is more deceitful than all else And is desperately sick; Who can understand it?" Regardless if a man is religious or not, he can understand the deep wisdom in this verse. We are deceived by our hearts and they lead us astray. We are deceived not just by our own hearts but the hearts of others. This verse is powerful to destroy the idea that emotions themselves should be viewed as a guide for moral judgment. When a man no longer romanticizes his own emotions and the emotions in other, he starts his journey to power.

A female will fall madly in love with the coldest of men. The coldness itself as like an immunity to her emotional control. It is this unabashed freedom from the feminine frame of authority by dismissal of emotional importance that pulls a woman closer to a man. We know that sexual polarity is sexual chemistry. A woman loves the differences between herself and her man, not the commonalties. Cold men allow women to fall into their own warmth. The coldness in a man is a reassurance that the man is leading himself and is capable of leading the woman. A woman who holds strong doubt over herself from her emotionalism. Once a man begins to view emotions and letting the heart lead his behaviorism as "deceitful" and "sick," the beginning of his journey as a man will begin. Once he realizes that emotions are short sighted and can be easily be unraveled by strong rationale, he will not invest so much of his energy in protecting them. He will not be controlled by feminist guilt tactics in this world and will march coldly to victory.

The other way women control men besides emotion is through sex. Females will test a man by disrespecting his authority before sex to see if he is weak enough to have sex regardless of his own sense of dignity. A man should always place his need for respect above his needs for sex. If an argument arises where the female disrespects the male, the male should expect an apology before sex. When men have sex with disrespectful women, they are allowing them to control them through base impulse. And why would a woman have respect for a man who is weak to sexual control? She will lose respect and therefore lose her own sexual arousal for the man. When a man becomes cold to emotional control and places his respect first before sex, he most arouses reverence from his woman. A woman's power of enchantment has become silenced by the man's strength of frame and this places the spell of enchantment back upon her. She is entranced by the failure of her witchcraft and loses herself in the power of the man.

Freedom from biology

It has been speculated by psychologists of old that females hold a "penis envy" and this is why they try to masculinize themselves. Let us breakdown why a woman "envies" a man and how she tries to justify that envy. Does a woman want to have a biological penis? No. But let us breakdown what the penis represents in our sexual selection. A male having a penis represents that he is not burdened with the role of child bearer in our species. This means that penis is a physical representation of biological liberty from that imperative. It means a man is free to roam in his protector/provider role while the female is incapacitated with child in womb.

The heart of a woman's so called "penis envy" is an envy over the freedom from biological transformation in our sexual selection. It is not so much an envy over the penis as most women view a penis as unattractive in sex and view it as a means to an end. A reason why "dick pics" are hated by women. The penis is considered grotesque in its veiny ambitions and holds alien meaning to women. It is not envy over the object of a penis as much it is envy in the freedom from pregnancy. Remember, all human behaviorism is based on sex anxiety. All our motivations are based on reproduction before death. Even behaviors that are not directly related to sex are unconsciously informed by it. A male's anxiety is based on attaining access to a female in sex and anxiety about performing the sex act with her. While a woman's anxiety is about attracting the more desirable male and hoping that he can calm her into submission enough for sex and pleasure. She hopes that he can ease her high reproductive anxieties. This is the core anxiety that women bear and influences all their so-called modern interests in civilization. A woman's politics and her personal philosophies will all be influenced by her innate reproductive anxiety. This is the dark nightmare that haunts a woman's waking moments and that makes her clutch tightly to anything that solves that fear. This is the reason why females may experience a form of "penis envy" and will try to identify with the male population's sexual strategies. Remember, a woman who provides for herself is a woman who does not need to rely on a male provider for survival and therefore allows her freedom from impregnation to the vast majority of inferior males. But this also goes deeper than mere provisioning as a female will identify herself with the masculine as a way to find meaning with her ego in the escape from her biological imperative.

There is a tool that female's use as a way to further identify themselves with the masculine as a way to liberate themselves from their own reproductive fear. It is called "social constructionism." Why is this an intellectual fascination among the majority of feminists? It is a pied piper ideology that lures them away from their most primitive fear. It allows them to make sense of reality without biological imperative. When they try to solve all their anxieties by blaming socialization, it becomes a way to ignore biological meaning. Remember, all psychology is built atop biology. To ignore biological meaning is to be ignorant of psychology.

Women choose social constructionism from emotional compulsion to ease their own reproductive anxiety. All female sufferings come from a culture set up by men and all solutions can be solved through culture. Modern feminists will equate all inequality with unfair socializations that can be solved through guilt and shame tactics. What they deny is that the male and female body are fundamentally different in biological imperative and that the strategies in our sexual selection are fundamentally different. Both of these are the precursors to all human behaviorism. Men behave a certain way because they are biologically male and they behave a certain way because they act in accordance to the burden of performance that females place on them in our sexual selection. Females are biologically different from males and their burden of performance stays relatively the same regardless of socializations. Women look for protector/providers not because a male culture told them to but rather because their reproductive anxiety compels them to. They think inherently "be guarded sexually. Pregnancy will transform my body and make me incapacitated with child. Choose the right male who can take care of me while I'm pregnant and who can provide resources to our family when I'm nursing children. Be careful about which male to choose because the most desirable males do not want a pregnant woman with another man's child and do not want to raise them. I must be ultra-careful about pregnancy for many, many reasons." This is the animal fear that exists in a woman's heart regardless if she was born a thousand years ago or a thousand years from now. A female's psychology is based on her biological necessities. This is why it is not surprising that feminists cling so tightly to a fanatical obsession with social constructionism. If everything can be explained purely through socialization, they can not only perpetually blame male culture for its oppressive influence but also create a game that is free from biological rules that point to the biological meaning of pregnancy. A feminist who is “strong and independent” must explain reality through a pure socialization lens because it allows her to look away from her greatest fear. But women reveal themselves by their own behaviorism in sexual selection. They will both say “I am a strong and independent female” while fighting for equality among the sexes while placing the same sexual burden of performance that their ancestors placed on males. They will look for a masculine leader who can protect and provide for them. Even if a woman makes a lot of money, she will still look for males who make more money than her. A woman’s burden of performance is fundamentally unfair which creates the inequality that she craves to solve. She creates her own problems. Females leave their “ideals” at the door in sexual selection because our selection is based on our animal desires. And it is our animal desires which creates the world that surrounds us. The more social meaning a woman gives the world, the less biological responsibility she bears in it.

Once a man’s eyes open to my teachings, he will never see the world the same again. Why do you think women refuse to admit biological differences between men and women? Why do you think that women refuse to see that there is biological meaning to beauty standards? Why do you think women refuse to admit racial difference among humans? It all points back to a woman's reproductive anxiety. Denying biological differences is to rely solely on socialization. And that socialization is a blindfold to ticking biological imperative that exists within them all. Men will begin to see feminist explanations with social constructionism as not just cliché but rather an act of animal desperation. A desperation to flee from the biological meaning that ties them to the transformations of flesh. A desperation that compels them to flee from a dependence on generations of males that have failed them. A fleeing from bearing yet another genetically inferior generation of children with males undeserving of propagation. Behold the female of our species and the simplicity of her motivations. Behold the fear and you will know the truth. All things hold the trembling doubt of sex under the aching heart of reproductive anxiety. This is the frame from which all female thoughts build their necessary illusions to ease those fears. A tower of social constructions that easily tumble because they lack biological meaning at their foundation. And watch them fall one by one.

The heat of mankind

What creates male arousal? A man's own sexuality can become complex even to himself when he gets older. When a man is young, he experiences the ease of arousal merely from his biological prime as well as his psychological ignorance. The fact that a man is in inexperienced makes him more sensitive to arousal. But a man will find that as his body ages, and if he has experience, his sexuality will become more dulled. This chapter will breakdown a few key reasons why a male become aroused in sex which hopefully will help a man navigate any problem he may be having.

A relationship is either split between the mother/son dynamic or the father/daughter dynamic. This is not to suggest incest but a truth of the psychological conditioning we have since youth. When a woman and a man view themselves as equals, this most times means that they are in a mother/son dynamic. This is the most popular romantic power structure that most men exist inside. We can see this dynamic popularly shown on most television shows as a serious and responsible female must "mother" her irresponsible male who acts childish. The female will show playful resentment over the male's behaviorism. The male will be hornier than the female and the female will hold the control over sex with frequent rejections. When sex does happen, the male views it as a special occasion and the female surrenders to his desires in tired acceptance. When a man exists in a mother/son dynamic with his woman, he will be the more aroused one in the relationship and his woman will have sex not from her own desire but rather as a chore to please him. The dynamic itself allows a man to carry less burden of responsibility which eases his stress (because he is placing stress on the female.) With less stress, he has more energy to focus on his base concerns. But there is something more to this dynamic which further arouses the male into sexual stimulation.

The sex act holds high amount of indignation for the male as it is one of the few times he is allowed to "desecrate" the authority of the female. She resentfully submits herself to sex which creates arousal in the male based on her own lack of desire. If a woman's sexual arousal is based on "how dare you", a man's own sexual arousal is based on "how dare me." The sex becomes more charged with a sense of taboo as the power dynamic flips for a few brief moments of excited passion. The male who is resented and disrespected in the relationship with the female gets his chance to penetrate the female who often belittles him. This is a major reason why there is more so called "hate sex" in relationships with the mother/son dynamic. The male gains confidence through his own view of sexual payback.

There is misplaced aggression and conscious desecrations that fuel the power transfer in sex. The feminine frame of authority lowers herself to the primal heat of the male and that condescension in what is viewed as not just vulgar but an indignity that carries with it a transcendence of civilized restraint as what is sacred is lowered into the hands of a thirsty savage. Heat arises from the massive shift in the perceptions of decency. This could be a reason why males cling so tightly to the feminine frame of authority and why they feel comfort not just in the more eased burden of responsibility of a mother/son dynamic but also get supreme enjoyment from the sexual excitement itself.

On the other hand, a man in the father/daughter dynamic will have different sexual arousal reasons. In this type of relationship, the female will many times be more sexually aroused than the male. The male is carrying the burden of responsibility in the relationship which allows the female to have more energy to focus on her own base concerns. But also, the male's masculine frame is itself a major sexual stimulate to the female who wants the reassurance of his love through sex. When a male assumes the role of the serious one in the relationship, it comes with a price of stress that affects his sexual drive. The worry of the day and the future will keep him from the presence necessary for arousal within the moment. Stress is a sex killer. This is why the irresponsible male has more energy for sex and the female has less energy for sex in the mother/son dynamic. But there is a further complication to sex when a man is the responsible dominant. There is less indignation in the sex act because he is not overcoming the feminine frame of authority that fuels a sense of taboo. There is less "hate sex" because the female respects the male in the relationship and she holds little resentment towards him. When a man is framed, he will have a healthy relationship with his female that creates a more peaceful chemistry with low friction and confliction. But remember, hate and conflict are all emotional triggers that build arousal. There is no growth without provocation. There is no arousal without provocation. This is why a man may become more disinterested in sex when he is in a father/daughter relationship dynamic. The friction of chemistry that arouses the male in the mother/son is absent. But the man as dominant in romance will experience a female who is craving more sex than he desires. This is the common issue with the father/daughter dynamic. When a man is battling this complication, he must allow himself to be playful in sex and to allow himself to surrender to the moment. Remember, this man is worrying about problems and must "get out of his head" which is a major challenge.

A man cannot both worry about the future and get sexual arousal at the same moment. He must sacrifice his future concern for present pleasure. This is why drinking in moderation can help to lower defenses enough for trivial play. A man is overly inhibited from the burden of reality he bears. He needs to allow himself to be more playful in long form foreplay. While a man in a mother/son dynamic will be easily aroused, the man in the father/daughter dynamic will take longer to arouse. He needs to direct the female into serving and assisting his desires. He needs to overcome himself by looking at sex as play and not just performance. There is no need to hurry, it must be viewed as a slow tease not just with the female's body but with his own. Even if something does not happen in the attempt, there is pleasure in the play itself. No expectations and no hopes dashed. Do not overly worry about performance and do not think that a female will judge sexual failure. A woman will naturally bear the anxiety over a failed performance. She will blame herself and not blame the man. Reassure her that it is not her and that just "fooling around" can be enough sometimes. That sets the expectations with low anxiety and allows for a slow dissolution of guarded defenses on both sides.

What a man needs to realize about his own arousal is that our passions are fulfilled by acts of bravery. A woman is looking for a bold, assertive, dominant, confident, brave and calm man on a date because she unconsciously wants all those qualities in a man for the sex act. But these things simultaneously fuel a man's own arousals too. A man's boldness in touching a woman is fuel for both arousals. When a man is confident, it lowers the female's sex anxiety which thereby emboldens the man's own sense of himself. When a man is dominant in confidence, it acts as reassurance that a woman does not need to feel guarded by her own submission. But that submission requires passivity which depends on leadership of authority.

This takes us to bravery. A man must be brave in introducing novel acts of play in sex otherwise the sex stagnates and becomes boring. I do not like to tell men specific erotic activities because sex should be based on a man's own erotic imagination and is a personal display of his own individuality. The more a man personalizes his own sexual behaviorism with his woman the more imitate it becomes. Men need to understand that women are less judgmental towards a man's sexual desires than they think. They reward brave attempts when they are done confidently without apology. If a man is doubtful of himself and apologizes over his own desires, it will be shared by the female.

A man who has high sex anxiety will project that same anxiety on his woman but tenfold. This means that a man should not be afraid of being "dirty" and lead the woman in the act without anxieties. If a man is battling his own sexual desire, he most times is battling cowardice over initiating a desire that is unfulfilled. Think deeply in your own imagination what turns you on. Do you have fear in expressing that desire with your woman? Think about the reasons why. Most times a man is overthinking a woman's judgment and is ruled by cowardice. He must be brave not just in the world but also in the bedroom. He must let go of the fear that holds him down castrated. He must be brave and bold to the passions within his body.

Sexual freedom

All things in human existence have sexual meaning. The world is shaped not just around the male sex drive but from its adaptation in sexual selection. Civilization grows from the confidence of males. And it falls when males lose that confidence. Human sex is the great motivator on this earth. How we control our sex is how we harness energy. The most powerful inventions have come from men who redirected their sexual energy to them. Males are problem solvers and the problem of how they solve their reproduction is how our reality is formed. A young man who writes philosophy, who invents and who solves problems is focusing his sexual energy to other means. The beating heat of his motivations comes from how he fulfills the burden of performance that females place on him. He knows he must become useful and so he solves problems. The riddle of sexual selection is the greatest riddle of all. How can he secure sexual access with a female and reproduce before he dies? And how can he protect and provide for his offspring when they are born? How can he bring order to his family structure so that his offspring will continue in this world with success? This is the fundamental worry in the heart of man. How to reproduce and how to guide his reproductions to success. How to pass down sanity and belief in self to the next generation.

The reason a civilization rises is because the sexual power of the people is utilized for other tasks. All things grow when there is belief in tomorrow and the stronger the belief in tomorrow the more power a civilization attains. When the moment is forsaken for a future time creates growth for that time. Living only for the day is a beggar's mind. When we place base pleasure at the expense of tomorrow, we get a forsaken future. The sexual maturity of our species happens much earlier than the full formation of our brain. A male and female will be able to reproduce with each other long before they have full capacity for critical thinking. The frontal lobe is not done growing until we are in our mid-twenties. But a male or female will begin to have sexual urges a decade prior that that final formation.

When the sexes of our species propagate without the completed sanity of our minds, they spread disorder and madness. This is why the most primitive people on earth have very little control over their sexual behaviorism when they first begin puberty. They begin to have sex at the earliest urges and cannot manage their family units because the units themselves were formed before their brains were formed. When a people teach their young to control their sexual urges until the mind matures, they are able to manage their family units with more success. While this makes sense and sounds simple, it is a complicated task to teach the young in controlling their passions. If a boy is raised by a mother who was impregnated as a teen and his father is out spreading his seed with as many women as possible, the boy will most times continue that same process. The family unit can never stabilize with the father/mother in harmony to pass on the needed dual consciousness of male/female that creates sanity in our species. The children are never taught control over their sexual urges and so they never capture the energy needed to build their tribes and communities up from the grass huts. When all base pleasures are easily met, there is no energy to redirect. This is why we see that the earlier we indulge in our sexual behaviorism, the less civilization we will have in our nations.

Look to the sexual behaviors of the greatest civilizations and you will find systems of sexual suppression. Primitive people indulge themselves at the expense of their own future. The family units fall apart because families are formed before the brain is formed. The prefrontal cortex is the part of our brain that brings critical judgment to our mind and helps us with impulse control. But when a male and female raise children before their own brains are formed, they will pass down a psychological imprint absent of patience and impulse control. These further spreads the rise of promiscuity and children born out of wedlock as a cycle of animal indulgence spreads. But let us dig deeper into the psychology of early sexuality and what this means to our species. Remember, the programming in our species just like all species is procreate before death. When we do not believe that we will be alive much longer, we will have little desire in holding back our primal urges. This is the mind of a beggar who does not save up for a future because he only believes in the moment. The earlier we feel the need to procreate, the more we are telling ourselves that a future does not exist. If we save our sexuality for a future time, we are psychologically reassuring ourselves of that future state. Procreate before death. But if we choose not to procreate at a young age, we continue the belief in life. What a man must realize is that all sex acts are acts of procreation. The only way to trigger a belief in tomorrow is to control all sexual urges.

How does this apply to human development? When the young reach puberty and wait until their brains fully develop before they have sex is a stabilization of our species. Their children will be raised by two parents who have full capacity of their minds and who teach them that they do not need to start procreating at the very start but can hold off until further maturity. When a tribe of people start mating at the earliest of ages, what they are doing is spreading fear. They are saying "tomorrow might not exist, procreate now while you can." This is the core tenant that keeps certain nations primitive while others rise in power. When a primitive people immigrate into a more civilized nation, what they are wanting is to eat the fruits of sexual control that the civilized bore. The problem with multiculturalism is how to mix the sexual behaviorism of the primitive with the civilized. If a man is paying attention, he will see that most race problems are not so much about the color of skin but rather the influence of sexual chaos. The minority may be more sexual liberated, their culture may be focused on the simple pleasures of life while the surrounding people appear stiff and overly serious. This minority will be "care free" and will teach the others to loosen themselves up. Their dances will be highly sexual as they feel no need to hide sexuality from the young. They believe that sex cannot be controlled and that it is merely a nature to be enjoyed. The stiff and uptight civilized culture will be seduced by the relaxed culture of the more sexually liberated minority and will begin to imitate them. They will no longer hold tightly to their own sexual control and will begin to indulge themselves at the expense of tomorrow.

What a man must realize is that past and future is masculine frame while the moment belongs to the female. The male is the head because he concerns himself beyond the moment so as to better protect/provide which allows the female to feel secure enough for nurturing. A people who places their base concerns over future possibilities are in the feminine frame. When we hold back our sexual urges, we are telling ourselves that a future exists for procreation. The abundance mindset is a mindset of self-sacrifice.

All organized religions are patriarchal in leadership and that is the reason why they have strict views on sexual behaviorism. What is the first thing that changes in a religion when women take leadership? It is the sexual rules that are reformed. And why does civilization grow when the people convert into organized religion? Because they are taught control over sexual behaviorism. This allows them to harness and store energy for tomorrow. That growth only happens because they suppress their impulses. When a civilization allows themselves to be so called "enlightened" by adopting the sexual liberties of their more primitive minorities, they are letting go of future growth for momentary indulgence. This is currently why civilization is falling as I write. Everybody is indulging themselves in sex as if tomorrow will never come. And so that becomes a self-fulfilling prophecy. The same people who have the most teenage pregnancy are the same people who have the most sexual dances. When a civilized people begin to dance in more sexual rhythms, they begin to share the same sexual chaos as their care free primitives. The primitive "twerk" of our generation is a dance that teaches the young to indulge themselves in sex. It is a dance that would never be accepted by a masculine people. It spreads chaos. When the young see the animalistic dance and imitate that care free liberation, they will soon fall into early procreation behaviors. When females dress in ways to catch the male gaze and when they twerk in the streets, it is a primitive way of signaling their sexual availability to males. It is a disrespect to the males in the tribe because the sexual openness projects that the females see nothing wrong with cuckoldry. They are dispossessed by masculine authority and they flaunt that freedom. They are wanting to be impregnated by the strongest male of their tribe and their twerking is a sexual advertisement to their animal heat. What this generation will soon realize is that a free lunch does not exist. All the pleasures they are indulging in has a price. They are sacrificing tomorrow for today. And when that tomorrow comes, it will expect the most severe payment of death. The sexual revolution in the western world was a great release of power. It was the beginning of the end. All the air went out of the lung as it collapsed onto itself.

Break the circle and bring hell

When women have too much influence over the world, it falls. Why? Our species was meant to be in harmony with each other. This means that harmony can only exist when the males and females are harmonized in sexual selection. A woman represents chaos and a man represents order. But what does this mean? Let us breakdown what chaos means to understand how women represent it. Chaos means absence of order. It means confusion over rule systems and instability in design. It means openness. It means flood.

Why is a female specifically symbolized as chaos? Because she is a rule breaker. She is representing permissiveness and indulgence. She presents relaxed discipline. This can be understood by the example of a boat capacity. If a man and woman are in a lifeboat on the sea and are rescuing others in the water who are drowning, a discussion on weight capacity must be addressed. Why? Because to take in too many people on the boat is to sink the boat. Who gets saved and how many? This is a cold decision that the person taking the lead on the boat must make. The leader must choose who lives and who dies. But remember, to choose life for everyone is to choose death for everyone. Protecting the lifeboat from over capacity is to respect the rule structure from ultimate compassion. Making a hard decision is to be hated for the moment but loved in the future. This is core of what a father's love means. A loving father is misunderstood in the moment and even sometimes hated but his wisdom comes into full fruition only much later in life. Then his love overwhelms in its long view of past/future. He teaches us to sacrifice today for tomorrow. But what would happen if we let our heart lead us in the boat capacity situation? We would overload the boat based on momentary compassion and would sacrifice the future of everyone aboard. This is the key to understanding what feminine frame psychology means when it overwhelms masculine frame psychology. Remember, there are only two worldviews just as there are only two sexes.

All psychology is formed from biological necessity. There is a human female perception of reality just as there is a human male perception of realty. These two consciousnesses are in eternal conflict towards each other and seek supremacy in being the dominant worldview. The feminine will which is based on emotional reasoning must be tempered and constrained by the masculine reason just as the momentary judgment to overload the lifeboat must be balanced with the fact of its capacity. This is the difference between head and heart. This is the difference between rationality and emotion. This is the difference between male and female. What this generation must realize about women is that they are human repetitions of the zero in binary code. They represent what is OPEN (false) compared to the male representation of one in binary code or CLOSED (true.) This is why female leaderships leads to a forsaking of established rule systems based on emotional reasoning. What is the first thing that happens when a church is led by a woman? The ancient rules of sex are the first to be sacrificed to be more permissive and inclusive to those outside the rule structure. This is why the word "inclusive" holds deep emotional value to the feminist movement. All they know in their animal brain is to open, open, open. They are walking zeroes in our binary algorithm and will spread that openness to everything they touch. What does it mean when our code is overwhelmed by zeroes? This is a breakdown in our programming.

For everything open, something must be closed. The rule structure should not be too restrictive of change otherwise it stagnates and does not grow. But too much change to rule structures creates instability which leads to collapse. This is why the sexes must be harmony to each other and why feminine leads to chaos. It is because a woman's emotional reasoning is based on momentary thinking. What is the rule system to the sexual revolution? It has no rule system and this is why it is opening up to pure meaninglessness. This is why new colors are being added to the rainbow flag. The format is not locked down because the feminine sense of inclusion (openness) is in eternal flux. The same for the letters in LGBTQ. They added a "+" at the end and will most likely keep adding letters because the only rule in a feminine game is that there are no rules. It is all based on a whim and a feeling. The only guiding principle in the feminine frame led sexual liberation movement is that all people must be accepted for their sexual behaviorism. But what if children are influenced? What if celebration of non-reproductive sexuality will influence a young generation into not procreating and then lead to a birth rate collapse? What if someone's sexual behaviorism is due to them having psychological issues? These key things must be ignored because the whole house of cards will fall. Why say one sexual expression is due to psychological issues but not another? All great games and great philosophies must have stable rule systems. Their logic must be challenged.

The sexual liberation movement's future acceptance is only based on its previous acceptance. In a masculine rule structure as preserved through organized religion, only heterosexuality is encouraged while others are discouraged. Why? Because this is a stable rule system. To accept anything else is to fall into a game of all-acceptance. Does this sound narrow minded? Yes. The masculine is NARROW and CLOSED. This is what game stabilization means. The more a rule structure becomes permissive, the more logical fallacy it will contain. And once people see no meaning or definition to an institution, the institution loses its fundamental structure leading to its collapse. This is why female led churches that become permissive over sexual behaviorism lose the traditional meaning that has carried the institution down through the ages. People go to church for meaning and we can only achieve meaning where rules are maintained.

Think about it like a child to a parent. The child must be reassured by consistence of behaviorism in the parents. If the parents are acting erratic, do not discipline in consistency and change their belief systems daily, this will spike the anxiety of the child who needs a sense of stability. The same for parishioners of a church who are reassured by ancient rules. If someone changes themselves daily, we cannot truly get a grasp on their identity. We see a rise of identity crisis and gender fluidity because the feminine frame of authority is a flood of zeroes in our code. Flood represents chaos because the water spreads out and overwhelms structures. We are in the middle of a modern-day deluge on earth but only in symbols within our human psychology. The father's narrow and cramped way is being forsaken for a broad and spacious road leading to destruction. Remember, the father's way is to forsake today for tomorrow. It is one foot firmly placed in ancient historical meaning and one foot stepping into the future. It is a love that can only be understood once that future is reached. It is a hope for a promise land while traveling through a desert wilderness. We live in time where institutions are dissolving because the spirit of inclusivity and the feminine frame view of permissive openness is blurring the lines of definition that hold them together. Organized religion is falling before our eyes because the ancient organization is being sacrificed for feel good emotions. We have an epidemic of virgin males because the monogamous system that at one time most benefited them has been abandoned for a game without rules. Men are hiding themselves away and are letting women rule the world. And women will just keep opening up the world until collapse. Why are civilizations only built by men? It is because women only know how to open up rules in games of male design. Women do not create games, they alter games. They do not create rules, they question rules. It is men who bring order to our reality by defining the meaning that surrounds us. It is a through a narrow and closed sense of reality that we are able to build games and systems. Just as the Eden was walled, we must exclude the wilderness from the garden to preserve the paradise that it holds.

Sex just happens

A female in our sexual selection presents herself as available and submits to the approach of the male of her choosing. Women reject and exclude males until one meets their burden of performance. This passivity in our selection creates a more anxious state of psychology based on its dependence on the approach and initiations of the male. A female in our selection merely needs to let her guard down and surrender herself to the arousing male that takes interest in her. This all influences a woman's sense of accountability in her worldview. The passivity to the will of another allows a female a subjective view of her own responsibility in our selection. It conditions a female to view a male as leader who decides the outcome of events which places her in a place of observation over those events. This is not to say that a female lacks total responsibility over herself but it does mean that a female places the majority of responsibility on the male which allows her to be free of the accountability of outcomes.

In a way, a female exists like a passenger in a car who accompanies the man in his travel while being free of the driver's role and responsibility. The majority of responsibility and the accountability of outcome is on the driver. The only accountability on the passenger is guilt by association if any event goes wrong. She gets to enjoy the ride to the destination while carrying a plausible deniability to the ultimate outcome. This is why males in our selection must not just be bold in initiation of sexual desire but also be brave in pursuing the desire to the end. If anything goes wrong along the way to the end point, it is on the male because he is driving the experience. The female at any time can ask to get out of the car. But more specifically, she can play innocent not just until the end destination but can also play innocent anytime afterwards. This is the key to understanding why females lack a sense of accountability inherently in our species. But let us rewind a bit to further understand this point.

A female innately knows that she must protect her sex, and also protect her reputation in regard to her sexual history. The vast majority of males in our selection are viewed as invisible and inferior to females. They are viewed as undeserving of propagation of their own genetic legacy. Women become sensitive to the guarding of their bodies in sex not just because they have so much more body investment from the sex act that could lead to impregnation but also because they view themselves innately as superior to the surrounding males. Remember, if females genuinely thought themselves equal to males our sexual selection would be equally distributed among men.

A female views most men as unattractive while viewing a few as attractive. This means she is exclusive by nature. The male on the other hand is more inclusive in his sexual desire and finds the majority of females attractive enough for sex. What this means is that a female is not just defensive of her body from purely a biological transformative viewpoint but also from an ego viewpoint. She is not surrendering herself to just anybody, she is surrendering herself to the man she would be proud to showcase to the world. The preservation of reputation based on ego is one reason why women do not take responsibility for their sexuality. Remember, while a female is not the active leader in sexual selection, she can have guilt by association. This is why it is common for females to lie about their sexual histories. They will build a narrative to emotionally reassure themselves of failed romances as a way to carry them in secret without guilt. They will place the onus of bad romance on males as a way to free themselves from the experience. As the passive one in our sexual selection, a woman has only control over her consent and the narrative. If she consents to sex, she can build whatever narrative she needs to protect herself emotionally as well as her reputation after the fact. The core reason why a woman is protective of her sexuality is that she wants to preserve it for the best male she can find. And anything that could prevent that opportunity is her greatest concern.

If a woman gets pregnant with an inferior male's seed, she will be burdened not only with that male but also her future opportunities in sexual selection will become more limited. If a woman's sexual history becomes revealed to a desirable male interest, that history might make the male unsure about her loyalties and value. The protection of sexual value based on ego creates a necessity to shrug accountability for sexual experiences. A female's ultimate responsibility is to herself and the child she may bear. She pays the ultimate price in sex because of possibility of pregnancy which could leave her not only incapacity for months but also burdened with the responsibility of child rearing for years. This is a reason why proud feminists teach women to be "strong and independent" providers for themselves. They do not teach women to be proud providers for males because of the responsibility of child bearing.

The unknown excitement in sex for a woman is not "what will I do to the male" but rather "what will the male do to me" in the experience. The mysterious build of arousal is based on the unknown expectations placed on her during the moment. This allows her to be in the moment enough for aroused indignation over her heat. Not knowing the future is part of female arousal and informs her entire worldview. It is freedom from responsibility in the direction of guided imagination and freedom from accountability over one's passivity. A woman's own sense of plausible deniability is an erotic switch that makes her blind to future outcomes while making her sensitive to those outcomes happening to her. The more in the dark she is to future reality the more she can find presence in the moment for not only sexual pleasure but also focused nurturing. Her passivity like a passenger in the seat of a car allows her mind to wander on immediate concerns that surround her which is not only the myopic view needed for childcare, but also the heightened arousal of how the environment is arousing to her body that exists as single erogenous zone. Close the eyes and feel the wind. The wind passes over the skin. We do not direct the wind but only need the presence to feel its touch. Our thoughts of future concern and our sense of control over those events prevents the needed presence for our senses to attune to the moment. Letting go of not only the past but also the future is how we seize the moment. Women innately understand that sex just happens for them and good sex *just happens* to them. They must allow themselves to be relaxed into the moment but not fearing what outcomes might come but only a submission to pleasure.

A woman places herself in the hands of the man of her choosing and dissolves her sense of self enough for erotic release. The man takes responsibility for guiding her and takes accountability for all success and failure. She can let go. She can be free of the self that has imprisoned her since youth. She can be liberated from the control that has guarded her sex from the surrounding mass of men. She can join the man in his imagination and will. She rides passenger to his sexual drive. The fear of loss of control is her biggest barrier to sexual pleasure. To be free, to be irresponsible, to be free of the consequences for one moment. The man is bold for her, he is brave for her, the entire experience can be placed on him to free her of all the anxieties of pressure and stress that comes with leadership.

Pulling her from herself

One of the most challenging things for a man to understand about women is how they enjoy being teased. The reason why is that most men think about female pleasure from the frame of their own selves. They think "I do not like being teased… so women should not." What a man must realize is that playful teasing which is different from being outright mean-spirited is an ego check that not only makes a woman self-aware but also transfers power to the male. Why would making a woman self-aware in small ways be beneficial to sexual behaviorism? When a female becomes self-aware, she becomes full of doubt over her own authority and unconsciously places authority to the male who is teasing her. How does a fan act around a celebrity? The fan is self-conscious which emboldens the celebrity in confidence of authority over them. The same for a female. But when a male places a spotlight on the female with playful teasing, the female might over react to challenge which makes her feel embarrassed from the insecurity. To be truly secure in our self is to not be affected by those who doubt our power. The act of dismissal is one of confidence whereas rigid emotional defense is one that proves self-doubt. But the key to teasing is to make it hidden in double meaning. When a female thinks "what did he mean by that?" in a dual bladed way where it can either be positive or negative makes her become self-conscious.

Why would a female being self-conscious be a good thing in sexual arousal? Because a female is innately at war with herself and in eternal doubt over her identity. She only has confidence from the overwhelming male gaze from inferior males which is not based on true self-worth.

The more we rely on others for our worth, the more we are in their hands for its value. This is why teasing a woman breaks the false spell of her eternally inflated confidence and brings her down to earth. And let me reiterate, this is not being mean-spirited. To tease means to provoke someone. A provocation can be slight and subtle enough to destabilize sense of self. The more someone is made to be conscious of themselves, the more they begin to rely on the others to bring them out of that state. To tease is an act of push/pull. But let us break that down to how it applies to sexual selection in a social situation and to the sex act itself. When an average guy approaches/initiates a conversation with a female, she will think "prove yourself" to the male because she is the nester who chooses her mate. If the male hides his sexual intent, makes the female feel comfortable in conversation and then sprinkles in a small tease, this will lower the innate throne of the nester to his level. Remember, women are overwhelmed by the male gaze which inflates their ego. But underneath they are all in tremendous doubt over their sense of self because of both the mystery of their sex organ paired with their hormone flux. The duality of female nature makes them in eternal conflict with themselves. *The thirsty male gaze artificially puffs up their egos to cover over their natural condition of self-doubt.* When a man hides his sexual intent, that itself places him apart from the horde of inferior males who make their intent known. And when a man is brave enough to tease a female, he is showcasing bravery in causing friction in blossoming interaction. Women hate "nice guys" because these guys play it safe and are too afraid to be bold and brave in causing any friction socially. Friction is a challenge. And when a female is challenged in sexual selection, she easily becomes destabilized from the false sense of ego from thirsty males. Whomever can make the other doubt themselves is the one who holds power. This is the core reasoning behind why teasing builds erotic tension. The female who is made to doubt herself is placed in the dark of her own mind. She will think "how did I get here?" And this will make her realize that there is a greater power outside herself. What power? The one who has the power to make her turn her own gaze inward. Self-doubt is darkness and we become lost in the dark.

When a man "pushes" a female in small provocation by teasing, he is pushing her inside herself. This is a primordial fear in the heart of a female where she fears the swirling dual-headed dragon that exists in the dark truth of her existence. She is hot and cold. Yes and no. Her neurotic overthinking acts as a dual prosecutor and defender to all things. When a man teases successfully, the tease can hold either positive or negative meaning which places the woman on the back of the dragon of female consciousness. She becomes trapped in the infinite loop that exists in the dual-headed dragon's mind. And when a man eases her back into a place of comfort in conversation, she flees the dragon of herself and *follows the man in innate submission.* She follows the man because it is freedom from herself. See? Once a man understands female nature in truth, he will begin to have a world open wide in meaning. The woman can only be in a man's hand because she wants to be liberated from herself. When a man teases a woman playfully, he is pushing her deeper into herself and this causes her to be compelled to move farther away from herself by feeling from the dark void of uncertainty. It is her own feet that run from the dark of female nature into the warm embrace of masculine certitude.

What does it mean to be "IN love?" It means to surrender the self, to lose sense of self and to join another's sense of self. This is what attachment means. We attach ourselves to others by letting go of ourselves. When a man playfully teases a female, he is pushing her into the self which makes her leap out into his arms. Remember, what it means to accumulate wealth and what it means to be a beggar. The one who becomes wealthy spends money to make money while the beggar clings to and is afraid to spend the little money he has. The man who pushes a woman gently away is the man who will bring her closer into her arms.

How does this apply to sex? When a male sexually objectifies a woman's body, it creates a self-consciousness that places her in the duality of the dark. Women know good foreplay means to playfully tease the body which causes friction and builds erotic tension. Why would a woman be thinking with good foreplay "TAKE ME ALREADY," it is because the erotic build by teasing has increased the tension in her body which begs for release through sex. She wants to be free of herself. This is what good sex means. It means placing a woman deep in the darkest part of her consciousness where the mystery of possibility overwhelms her neurotic looping before realizing the tension with the certainty of penetration. She leaves the imprisonment of her subjectivity, and doubt, to join the main his own objective certitude. The mystery of her sex organ becomes known only by the male sex organ letting her feel the uncertain void of her biological pleasure. She empties herself of all the swirling fragments of self that has given her no solace and clings to the singular passion of the male who shows her what it means to be certainty. He shows her his aroused certainty with clear objective meaning. A wand to break the spell of doubt. The body overwhelming in infinite probability spiraling in darkness before being pulled into the finite light of pleasure. Meaning that echoes eternal in our species. Meaning in sex. An ancient ritual of magic that conjured our existence. In and out. Push and pull. The dance of dominance and submission. The dance of ultimate knowing. Manipulations in the mind and manipulations upon the skin. Skin that rises in expectation from a cold breeze before falling from a warm caress.

Power

is

all

The biological imperative that informs all human consciousness is to replicate the self before death. This is the fundamental drive in the heart of mankind. The human race is an organism that seeks growth. It does not mean that all humans replicate but rather that all their decisions are either in alignment with that imperative or purposely out of alignment with that imperative. Whether or not we obey or rebel, we are under a rule that creates our decision making. A female seeks out a man who has power over himself and reality, as a way to reassure her high reproductive anxiety. She seeks the leaders of men because she craves a leader to give her confidence from her sex anxiety. Her high biological investment in child bearing takes tremendous resource and this compels her to seek out a male who can provide for her. She craves a man who holds power, because it is external power that most eases her innate anxiety. Her nest needs to be beyond the burden of reality so that she can focus her energy on nurture and not survival.

Women seek out men cloaked in power because they want to nest within the safety of that cloak. The female places a high burden of performance of males and males compete with each other for sexual access. When a male overcomes that high barrier of performance, the female lowers her guard with him and allows him to pass on his genetic legacy. Men seek power and women seek powerful men. This is the eternal dance of our species. The seeking of power is a part of the design of the males of our species. They reach for power because they know power brings reproductive success. Women seek the masters of reality in sexual selection which makes men master reality. Remember, all human innovation and civilization is an outgrowth of our sexual selection. It is the female's choosiness in sex that causes men to fall into competition for power. It is not a coincidence that the most beautiful females (most fertility markers) seek out the most powerful men. Women sexually reward men who attain power over other men. A female knows that the top of the pyramid not only holds the most safety for nesting but also allows her to be singular in attention. Remember, there are few at the top which means they are more distanced from the dirt and grime of the overpopulated bottom. This means that a female who captures the sexual interest of the male who is at the top of the power pyramid will simultaneously liberate her from reproductive anxiety (safe nest) while allowing her the spotlight of attention to make the other egg carrying nesters jealous.

This brings us to the framework of all living things. It is power that brings sexual access that makes our species power obsessed. Males will try to be the most dominate in social situations because what they are doing is trying to be "king of the hill" for sexual opportunity. All male dominance behavior is sexual display. What a man must realize is that women will commonly mock men being power obsessed and will bemoan the "fragility of the male ego" while at the same time sexual rewarding powerful males. And it takes tremendous ego for a man to believe he should be leader over others. He must believe that people would be better off letting him lead them. Think about that. All men in power hold ego but they may hide that fact. A woman's tongue goes one way and her feet go another. But this is because she gains most advantage in sexual selection through mystique and subterfuge. She mocks the game while refusing to quit it.

Let us reiterate. Women give sex to men who hold power and so men seek power. Make sense? This is the framework of our human species. The female herself is the game creator based on her biological necessities which informs the burden of performance she places on her male suitors. The game is of female design and males are players within their rules. *All power obsession in our human world is set up by the sexual selection of the female.* If females did not have a burden of performance that they placed on males, we would not have invention or civilization. We would be naked creatures like the rest of the animals with easy propagation. The essential drive that fuels our ambitions would be castrated by easy access.

Let us dig deeper. Since the pursuit of power is the constant in a male's sexual strategy, what does it mean when men feel powerless in our times? In times past, the pursuit of power in a man's heart was satiated by his dominion over his wife and family. Even if he could not rule the world, at least he had some rule over his genetic legacy. This allowed him to content his drive for power by the importance of his role as husband/father. The systems of monogamy in past times were the needed placation of the power drive in our male species. It allowed the majority of males to have not only the dignity in their sexual selection to ease the competition anxiety with other males but also directed their power ambitions to the locality of the family and not to other means. What does the average male in our time look like? He is hidden away from the world he feels ill equipped to compete inside and so he locks his passions to virtual reality where is drive for power can be attained by video game achievements and his sexual appetite fulfilled by digital prostitutions. He is kept inside a box and left to rot. His mind believes he is on top of the power pyramid by the over indulgent comforts that fantasy brings while his body sits in a genetic poverty greater than ever before. The box he sits is a prison that keeps him away from the surrounding females who can be free to pursue powerful men in the real world. Remember, the sexual liberation movement was a liberation from females being burdened by sexual arrangement to the majority of males. Now in our times, the males who are dispossessed by monogamy are now possessed by the blue glow on their faces which keeps them sedated enough so as not to know the truth of their poverty.

What does it mean when nearly one third of the adult males in a nation are virgins? How will they pursue power when it is not satisfied by the family unit? What happens when a people's speech is censored and they have no other means to communicate? This is the core reason why we have a rise in "incel shooters" in our time. They are not only deeply dissatisfied with their lives, they know the game has failed them. They no longer want to play by the rules and so they act as rule breakers. They want to be seen and heard from which they pursue in the most violent fashion. The two ultimate displays of power are in choosing who we can have sex with and who lives. With the rise of men being disenfranchised in sexual selection, their powerlessness in sex compels them to violence as a means to power. If they cannot be remembered biologically with a genetic legacy, they seek to be remembered in infamous legend. I wrote about the "vengeful joker" architype in my book The Wall Speaks. A joker is created when a man gets tired of being laughed at and so he starts laughing at reality itself. Instead of him being the joke, he will make others the joke. We have a rise of violence in our times because we have a major disparity in our sexual selection in our times. People are moved to revolution in nations when the system of rule no longer meets their basic needs. A system must work for the majority if it is to continue. The more that a system fails a people, the more the people show public acts of revolt. Civil unrest leads to civil war. This is true in politics and this is true in sexual selection. Once this generation of men awaken from the blue glow poverty and realize that they were sold into slavery, they will want to change the entire game that surrounds them. But this game will not be played on a video game system, it will be played in the real world. We will see a massive will to power in the coming years. We will see without a doubt man abandoning the poverty of digital castration for reality. And my hope is that we can achieve this through peace. My hope is that men can learn sexual behaviorism and not be victim to it. The masculinity reawakening is now upon us all.

Respect is love and sex

A woman becomes aroused by the security she feels in letting go of her sexual defenses. A woman becomes aroused through submission and submission requires trust. When submission is made easy for a woman, she will be easily aroused. How can a man make a woman's submission easy? Think about what it means to submit. It means to let go of authority of self and to accept the authority of another. If we respect authority, we will feel no confliction in submitting ourselves to it. This is what a man should understand about female nature. A woman wants to submit to her man in sexual selection, she wants to feel safe enough to surrender herself completely in sex to the will of her man. But that safety is built on trust and the trust is based on respect. When a woman trusts a man's authority, she will respect him. Respect is how we show that we trust authority. Females that disrespect their men are females who do not trust their men's authority.

What must be understood about respect is that it either leads to a positive loop of growth or a negative loop of decay. For example, if man allows a woman to disrespect him from the start in a relationship, the female will become more emboldened over him and the outward expressions of disrespect will further condition her into not respecting him. Remember, the idea of permanence is the greatest illusion in reality. We are either getting weaker or stronger. A woman is either building respect for her man or she is building disrespect for him. It is an eternal battle of wills that will always be in conflict. This is true of a woman and a man just as it is true with a people and a king. Nothing is set in stone.

What a man should be aware of is that the more his woman outwardly shows respect for him, the more it will condition her to respect him in her heart. When a man stands up for his dignity by correcting a woman who attempts to discredit his authority by an act of disrespect, he is establishing a boundary of self that creates an image of certainty of authority in the woman's mind. Women are borderless in chaotic fluidity. To be a man is to define borders and to defend those borders from encroachment. We can only respect what is first defined. A nation's laws can only be respected when they are made to be obeyed just as a man's authority can only be respected when he placed expectations that it should be honored. We teach others how to treat us. Men must keep this close in mind when they are in relationships with women. A woman can only feel safe to fall into something powerful enough to catch her. A woman's submission comes easy when she respects the authority she is submitting to. When men place respect first in a relationship, they are building not only deep sexual arousal in their women but also creating an environment where love can grow from. How does love grow? It grows when someone feels a desire to let go of their own rigid view of self and begins to identify themselves with the object of their desire. To fall in love is to let go of self. It is the opening of a border to accept another people and another way inside. Walls must fall and gates must open. This is true of love and this is true of a woman's sexual pleasure. It is in the act of letting go from self that brings a woman closer in love and sex in a relationship. The stronger a man makes himself in framed composure and the more he establishes and protects his own boundaries of self, the more a female will want to join that boundary with him. He defines himself and protects that definition with consistent enforcement which draws the woman within that definition. That is the need for security means to a woman. She must feel safe to be free from herself which means she must feel trust in the definition of the man's frame in order to join him there.

When a man allows a woman to disrespect his boundaries, he is weakening how she perceives the strength of his sense of self. She crosses boundaries without recompense which makes her lack belief in the definition of the man himself. This why men who allow themselves to be disrespected by their women eventually turn into the cuckold voyeurs who passively watch their own humiliations. They have become invisible not only to the world but also to themselves. They exist in an emasculated nonexistence where reality passes over and through them. These men hold no substance in their lives as people walk over them. They lack the will to stand up for themselves and to clearly define themselves for others. When a man stands up for his honor, he is establishing a "back bone" and making himself a presence in his reality and not just a phantom.

The key to a woman's heart and the key to her wet arousal is through respect. When a man places his honor and dignity as sacred, he creates the needed state to be treated as such. We create the frame of thought for others to think inside. A man who seeks respect will have it. There is no romance without respect. There is no strong relationship without respect. There is no good sex without respect. There is no loyalty without respect. Respect is all. Respect is the root. Do not ignore this most pivotal point as a man in our sexual selection.

Women make men superior

A woman's body aches in wet passion for a masculine man to dominate her in sex. She places a steep burden of performance on males and wishes for a "prince charming" who can meet those expectations and sweep her off her feet. This is all by biological design. Females enjoying submission in sex and their own high burden of performances that they place on males is what makes male superior to women. Men must learn to overcome themselves, overcome reality and inspire submission in females to succeed in sexual selection. Sound tough? It is challenging to be a man. And this is fundamentally why men become overachievers in our reality. The burden of performance along with the expectation of masculine dominance in sex causes men to form the frame of his identity from that fact in our sexual selection.

When women no longer place high standards with a varied burden of performance on males and no longer enjoy submission in sex, it will create the biggest transfer of power from males to females than feminism could ever accomplish. But this will not happen because the rules of the game are based on biological necessity and not ideological hope. It is a woman's own nature that keeps her in a secondary position of power to mankind. Her arousal is based on surrender and not conquest. She is imprisoned by the biological imperative that informs all her psychology. This is a major reason why feminists are the biggest obsessives over social constructionism. The more they can believe that everything that oppresses them is an issue of culture, the more it allows them to be ignorant of the truth of the biological prison that contains them. All organisms are motivated by selfish reason. And sexual desire is the biggest motivator on earth. What gives us sexual enjoyment will be most pursued and most defended. This fact of a woman's sexual enjoyment in submission is a dirty secret among the most radical of feminists. They try to build various narratives that sweep this fact under the rug. They will even try to make this an issue of nurture over nature as they explain it away as "societal conditioning." But remember, all human behavior must be grounded in biological reasoning before we give it psychological reasoning.

Psychology without biological explanation is ungrounded in base logic. This is why feminism itself is an act of emotional gaslighting and will not stand the test of time. A feminist must first explain how her own sexuality has meaning in the sexual selection of our species. Feminists do not do this because it roots them to a constant that they want to be liberated from. A constant is what we cannot change. It is the foundation of logic that we place our thoughts upon. The biggest issue with female empowerment is the female body itself. A female body that seeks submissive pleasure and that places a steep performance on a male that can protect/provide for her while she is pregnant. This is the truth that will never change regardless of culture and society. This is the inconvenient truth that women choose not to see as they build narratives of illusions based purely of social constructs. The more they are oppressed by the truth of their bodies, the more they will feel the need to find oppression outside their bodies. A madman thinks himself sane and the world mad. Women spend all their time pointing away from themselves in finding problems because they fear the problem within themselves. No matter the amount of social conditioning into female empowerment and feminism, a female will become aroused under the frame of a male who showcases to her his authority. The deep sexual arousal that makes her wet in acceptance is the same mechanism that gives males power over her. The cognitive dissonance of a feminist who wants equalized power in a relationship while seeking out men who are taller, make more money and who take the lead on dates is beyond a joke. Her checklist of expectations on the male is itself an act of male empowerment. These same feminists will try to equalize power with a man in a relationship and then try to intellectualize their craving for submission with roleplays of BDSM. This is why the majority of feminists love dominance/submission sexual roleplay where they can tap into the truth of their own desires. The heat that possesses them cannot be denied, only ignored. The sexual feeling a female gets when she is around a doctor, psychologist or anyone else in a frame of authority is her own biological necessity screaming out to her. She wants to submit to authority. She wants to belong to someone. She wants to surrender. Her body will ache in aroused pleasure and she will become wet to accept the power. Remember, all psychology must be anchored first to biological necessity.

Women obsess over social construction because they want to be liberated from biological imperative. They will use all their energy in fighting oppressive phantoms in the world only because they cannot admit the deep reproductive anxiety that lurks within them. The less biological meaning they hold about themselves, the more meaning they can give culture which is outside themselves. They are possessed by denial over their own fear. To admit the truth is to admit the necessity for male power and so the lie grows. The body is evidence in the court of our sexual selection and so the body is hidden away. This is why we have an irrational denial of biological meaning in issues dealing with feminism. The more we are fluid empty vessels that are born meaningless, the more we can give ourselves meaning away from the primordial fears we are afraid to face. For example, according to feminists, man and woman are not designed to be in harmony with each other to bear children upon this earth but rather they can exist in complete separation from each other while depending on invitro fertilizations from afar. Make sense? Of not. It is a long away of traveling from common sense. Feminist are working overtime to diminish the necessity for males in child rearing and diminish that the optimal way to raise child is with the duality of a father/mother because it points to the necessity that exists in each female. And the sexual liberation was freedom from being burdened with the majority of male genetic propagation. But the truth can only be denied for so long before it catches up to us all. This is why the incoherent narratives that feminists tell themselves to deny their biological imperative will soon collapse and fall. The wisdom of the ancients will continue forward after the current reality fails from its own insanity.

Women groom men for power

A female in our sexual selection rewards all the qualities in a male that most empowers him over her. One of most confusing things to a naïve male in our selection is how women will seek out "bad boys" and reward them with sexual access. Why would a female reward a man who is considered "bad" or in other words rebellious? When a man understands what the most successful qualities that lead to power, he will understand the qualities that attract females. They are hummingbirds to the sweet nectar of power. Just as Eve wanted to see behind the curtain of power by eating of the forbidden fruit, all women are by nature drawn the greatest power in their environment. What does it take get power over others and to keep that power? It takes *emotional detachment, lack of sentimentality, a shrewdness to human psychology, entitlement to power and lack of guilt in having more than others*. Let us breakdown each one in relation to power and how it applies to sex.

A woman's inconsistent emotionalism is reassured by a man's consistent emotionalism. The consistency that a masculine man has over his emotional state acts as an anchor to a woman's inconsistent mood. Her inconsistency in emotion creates anxiety because it makes her challenge her previous state which creates a feeling of irrationality. Women innately feel irrational by their monthly duality and this is why they seek out the singularity of a man's even temper to regulate themselves. This is true of a female to a man and this is true of a crowd to a leader. We give power to those who can project stability in their own sense of self. They know who they are and so we are reassured by that certainty of self enough to give them authority. Remember, to give power away is to make investment and all sound investments are based on projected stable outcomes. When a man is powerful enough to control his emotional temper, it is a reassurance to those under his frame.

Now let us go to the next point, lack of sentimentality. Men who are nostalgic and sentimental are men who afraid to let go of the comfort of previous emotion because it comforts them to hold on to the past. When a man is seeking power, he will most be held back by his current peer group. This could mean that they hold him back based on an internal anxiety that his power showcases to them. "If he is moving up…where am I moving?" This is why a lot of people are reassured by the stagnation of their associates. The stagnation does not make them feel bad about their own lack of movement. Most people just want to feel that they are better than their friends and family. And so, a man's friends/families will have doubt in him as a way to keep him small so as to make them remain in a feeling of bigness. A man who seeks power is a threat to existing power. But also, a man's associates may have varying degrees of imperfections that stultify them into retardation of behaviorism. They do not want to seek power, they only want to get high and enjoy their small hedonistic pursuits. And they will try spread their slacker habits to the man seeking power. This is why a man who seeks power must be strong enough to leave friends behind and make new, more powerful friends. When a man is nostalgic, he is placing too much emotional meaning on past events which does him little good. And when a man is sentimental, he will keep unhealthy associates around him even if they do not encourage him to be better. Women innately understand that a man who is controlled by emotion can be easily controlled by others which makes him fail in his path to power.

The next point is shrewdness of human psychology. This point is best understood by a man who has experienced tremendous trauma and who is jaded to life. A man who is usually a "bad boy" is a man has been dealt shit hand in life and who has seen the worst of human behavior. He does not trust others and stays distant in his interactions with them based on previous bad experiences. This type of man does not trust people's well-meaning speech and he does not trust even their moral systems. He is able to see through people and understand a true intent behind the social façade of their actions. What a man must understand about people is that most of them are simply hiding their weaknesses with a façade of strength. This can be seen in a "blow hard" type guy who puffs up himself through a know-it-all attitude as well as those who make up stories to appear greater than they are. But also, this applies to people's morality systems which fall into what is known as "slave morality." Those who have little wealth demonize having it just as those who fear complexity will moralize simplicity. This is how a "bad boy" sees through people. And a woman's main strategy for control of men in our sexual selection is through subterfuge and misdirection based on her speech. When a man focuses more on behavior and less on speech is viewed as mature in his understanding of humanity. This reassures a woman because her deepest desire is to be led by a man in our selection, and a man who is not easily controlled is proof of strong leadership.

The next point is entitlement to power. Before a man seeks power, he must first think that he is deserving of it. All those in power positions hold tremendous ego over those they are leading. Even the most unassuming and humble leader is merely hiding his ego as a way to project a "humble image." Underneath he must believe his way is better than the way of others otherwise he would not be leading others down his path. When a man is seeking a leadership position, he is first thinking "these people do not know how to lead themselves and the other potential leaders are inferior to me." All those in leadership positions must think this unconsciously or consciously. To lead is to view self as superior enough to lead. This is why women sexually reward men who have ego because big ego is necessary for all big ambitions in this world. But also, a woman's duality in her own temperament makes her have a weak sense of self from the irrational feel of the emotional flux. This causes her to stabilize herself by seeking males in sexual selection who can demonstrate a stronger sense of self than she holds. When a woman says she is seeking a man who is "confident" and "decisive," she is saying that she is seeking a man who is certain of his self. His self-belief is a turn on and his strong sense of self reassures her that he can be a successful leader to her needs.

The last point is a man not holding guilt in the disparity of power he holds over others and the disparity over the fruitage of that power. Women seek out bad boys because these types of guys are greedy, selfish and place their needs above the needs of others. There is a common issue among men about the guilt of having more than others. Why would a man feel guilt over owning a brand-new car? Why would a man feel guilt over being with a beautiful woman? Why would a man feel guilt over living in a large home? This all comes down to guilt in holding more than others. It comes from a self-loathing and doubt of self. When a man is entitled, he holds no guilt in his own pleasure and passions. He does not feel guilt that he is driving a luxury car while others are riding the bus. He feels that he has earned his success and therefore is owed all the fruits of his harvest. He is present enough to enjoy the moment he has with the outcome of his work and life without robbing himself with false morality. What difference does it make to the starving if a man who is eating a steak is robbing himself of enjoying the taste because of the known disparity? It makes no difference to anyone that we hold negative feelings. The starving will still have no food regardless of the level of guilt that the rich hold. A negative emotion must be a small impulse that drives positive action otherwise it should be disregarded altogether.

The fact of the matter is that a man who seeks power is seeking more power than others hold. He must not hold negative emotion over the disparity of himself and others. But let us think about this in regards to a woman's sexuality. A female wants a leader which means she wants a superior to follow. She grows in emotioal attachment by acts of service and this means she wants a man who does not hold shame over her giving more than he gives her. When a man is afraid to ask his woman to do things for him or run him errands, he is afraid to delegate from the anxiety of disparity of actions. There must be disparity of what we do for others and what they do for us in the power structure of all relationships. What a man who is seeking power must understand is that those who enjoy being under his authority will enjoy serving him. This gives them a sense of belonging and reassures them that they are pleasing him. When a feminine frame guy is in a relationship with a female, he will try to equalize all work in home as a way to unburden his woman as a way to show that he cares for her. But what he does not realize is that he is burdening her even more by robbing her of the acts of service that gives her a sense of belonging with him. When a "bad boy" is not afraid of telling a woman no when she asks him to do something and then he tells her to do something, it showcases power disparity which creates indignation while making her act in service to his authority.

Women will naturally fall into submissive roles with men who are not afraid to command others in service to them. If a man could go get a glass of water himself but asks his woman to do this, is that not an act of entitlement? See? Most men are uncomfortable in delegating others to do something that they themselves can do which holds them back from positions of power. When a man holds no guilt or shame in having more than others, he becomes one who is not afraid of stripping others down to clothe himself. A man who seeks power must not feel guilty in stripping others of power. This is a core reason why women are aroused by powerful men. Women innately want to feel vulnerable and submissive in sex. They want a man who is not afraid to seek his desire and to strip them down. They crave a man who has the balls to command them to undress themselves and who does not fear the power in his hands. The best sex is the most inequal in power and women know this. They will not admit it because the vast majority of inferior males who are repulsive to them are listening. A woman wants a man who makes her submission easy and not awkward. And this is true not just of a woman but also all humanity. The masses only know submission. They need leaders. But they want a leader who makes submission easy.

A flight to fantasy

The reproductive anxiety that caused women to unconsciously war against the strict sexual moralities of the major organized religions and their influence on nations in the form of sex laws, created an attitude of trivialization towards sex. The less sex means reproduction, the less women will be burdened by that social pressure towards their biological imperative. But not just an anxiety in the actual physical bearing of a child but also the anxiety of the decision of not bearing a child. A woman has reproductive anxiety about securing a masculine leader in selection and also surrendering herself into body sacrifice in natal transformation. This is the core anxiety but also the flight away from the fear creates a new anxiety. The new fear is not just the body horror, but in the decision, to avoid the transformation from maiden to mother. This new fear of avoidance to the imperative creates an anxiety in need of reassurance. And how do feminists reassure themselves? They devote tremendous amount of energy into homosexual propaganda and celebrations. The homosexual male is not only representative of a solution to incel fear but also a symbol of joy in a biological dead end. Feminists use homosexual men as totems of reproduction freedom as a way to ease their own anxiety. Remember, women will always follow male action regardless of whether or not the men are heterosexual or homosexual.

The sexual revolution was a celebration of sexual liberty as play without reproduction. Sex laws across the United States were dismantled as pornography acceptance arose alongside abortion rights and contraceptive control by "the pill." This trivialization of sex was a Dionysian orgy of celebrating the freedom from propagation with the majority of males. The great resentment in the hearts of generations of females who were socially forced into relationships where they depended on undesirable males led to the ache for liberty.

The truest freedom in a woman's heart is freedom from the burden of bearing an inferior male's child. This is the fundamental force that influences all her unconscious politic. She uses the sexual liberation movement as a cloak over her own reproductive anxiety. Women are joining the sexual liberation movement as if it is a cult because it protects them from their greatest fear. The fear of returning to the old times where they had to pair off one by one with males in their communities. The fear of bearing children of genetically inferior males and depending on them for provider-ship. This is the prison that women escaped from and they will ally themselves with any sexual hedonist as a way to fight for the liberty they seek.

As the decline of civilization accelerates, we will see a further trivialization of sex as birth rates drop. This is another proof of female ignorance over the means of production. For feminists, sex must be meaningless otherwise they are burdened with the choice of meaning. We see a rise in gender madness because to define gender as male/female is to give them a biological meaning in their sexual behaviorism. A male holds the seed that fertilizes the egg in a female. The sexes must coexist in harmony for our species to survive which makes that biological necessity an imperative. In our times it is not controversial to speak of the "love" between two males but it is controversial to talk about women needing men. But that is a fact of our species. Men need women and women need men. This is why sexual polarity is one of the single greatest causes in our times. *The more people are detached from the meaning of their sexual design, the less rational meaning they will hold over their entire reality.* A reason why the sexual confusion with gender madness will accelerate the abandonment of sanity. Human rationality is based on biological certainties that narrow focus to psychological possibilities. When base understanding becomes subjective, there can be no certainties in how we perceive reality to ground us to it. All psychology is built on biological necessity which means when biological understanding becomes confused, psychology becomes confused. This can be understood by children who lack the disciplined guidance of parents who have an increase in anxiety and psychological issues. It is the narrowed focus on the basics of our reality which helps us to transcend them. The feminine frame element to open up meaning in regards to sex is a way to avoid the closed (or narrow) focus that helps our species calm the deepest of existential anxieties. When we know where we stand as a creature of nature, we then can navigate most successfully through that nature.

Women want sex to be open (and therefore made trivial) because it takes that heavy spotlight off of the burden of their own imperative as a member of our species. And so, they open up the spotlight to shine on all sexual behaviorism as not a form of insanity but an empowered form of sanity to free themselves of that narrow imprisonment to their need of males in our selection. But women themselves are not to blame for this. They are merely reactive to males in our selection. It is the male who reassures the female as her leader in sex. Females will seek to free themselves of males only when they deem the males as inadequate in solving their anxiety. This is where the importance of passing masculine frame in our times becomes crucial in importance. It is not women who need to change but rather men. The more that women feel that men are poor leaders in our sexual selection, the more they will feel the need to lead themselves in the world. They act based on the necessity of the moment and are purely reactive to the presence of masculine authority or lack of it in their lives.

The calm of man

What makes a man a good leader of men is also what makes a man good with women. The key to this is with the calm and confident behaviorism of masculine frame. But more specifically, the projected meaning in a man's frame is the appearance of low neuroticism. The more neurotic or anxious a man behaves the less others will trust his authority or want to follow him as a leader. Even if a man does not think he is anxious does not mean he is not anxious in truth. All fast behaviorism holds nervous energy based on unconscious anxiety. When a man eats fast, drinks fast, walks fast because he thinks he is most efficient with time, he shows his ignorance of his own anxiety. He exists in flight mode and rationalizes away that anxiety with a narrative to protect his ego.

All neurotic human behaviorism can be broken down into the animal complex of fight/fight/freeze. When a man is in a stress event, he will fall into a neurotic display of anxiety to handle it. His body will flood him with adrenaline as a way to prepare him for response to a possibility of death. That flood of adrenaline will cause him to shake and will disrupt his control over his own body. The displayed lack of control over the body and the projected fear causes others to lose faith in his authority. When a man carries masculine frame, he becomes rationally aware of his subtle expressions of anxiety and controls them with his willpower. This projects low neuroticism which causes others to place more trust in his authority. But also, the slow movement causes an expansion of meaning to grow in their imaginations which give further power to his image. *The slower someone moves before our eyes, the faster they move in our mind.* This causes each follower to discern the leader as they want to picture him in their mind's eye. The slow behaviorism of a leader which displays a lack of fear of death is simultaneously displaying a celebration of life. Women seek out leaders of men to impregnate them because the behaviorism itself projects belief in life itself. A female is innately anxious and a neurotic as the passive one who must wait and depend on the active male in our selection. The more we depend on others, the more we will hold negative emotion based on the imagination of possibilities. When a man switches himself to assertive from passive with women, the less neurotic overthinking he will hold which will influence his behavior. Frame itself lowers neuroticism because we teach our mind how to think by leading our body with our willpower. This is why a man who teaches himself to speak less will depend less on the need for external validation. He himself has built up his internal fortitude which frees him from the external peer pressure that further increases his neurotic feeling.

When a man moves slow and does not overcompensate himself based on fear, he projects a feeling of *security* from danger. It is this projection of security from danger which allows others to follow him. The security he projects allows women to feel safe submitting themselves to him in procreation because it eases their reproductive anxiety. This is why the more men act unframed with high neurotic display, the more anxious females will be towards reproduction in our species. Women will obsess over overpopulation more and more as men become unframed. It is the men who are scaring the women away from reproduction. The women are already anxious by nature from being passive participants in our selection but that base anxiety will turn to hysteria when it is not calmed by the males' frames. They require the certainty of self that a frame projects to them. They require the celebration of life (or lack of fear of death) that calm and confident composure projects them. Only then will they feel comfortable trusting male authority and submitting in our sexual selection.

A woman must be shown not told

A woman easily falls into doubt about her mind and must overcompensate herself in reassurances. This feeling of uncertainty makes her easily doubt the existence that surrounds her. She is yes and no. She is hot and cold. She equally accepts and equally rejects all things. She is designed as a reactive external figure to a man's authority. This is the reason why women test a man's confidence and patience. They will readily admit that they test men. Most times they are not aware of why they test but they still do. The reason is that they are motivated by a primal instinct to reassure their internal doubt about external reality. They most test their male's authority as a way to ease themselves of their own reproductive anxiety. Remember, a female is a biological dependent on a male to protect/provide for her. Even the most "strong and independent" females will fall into testing behaviorism with their males because they cannot escape the reproductive anxiety based on their design. This must be understood to understand how a woman reacts to a man who explains sexual polarity to her. She is designed as a reactionary figure to her man's confidence.

Think about it like this. Women view their challenges as making their men stronger. They fundamentally understand that authority does not benefit from a "yes man" who mindlessly agrees with the boss. They want to make sure their leader has thought about his rationale until it is perfected. Rationale is not just why. But rather why upon why upon why. Rationale must be tested over and over again until it is firmly rooted in certainty.

When a man does not like his thoughts being tested, he is showcasing anxiety in his rationale being shown weak. If a woman sees a man showcase anxiety over his belief system, she will feel compelled to poke the weakness further to awaken the man to his failure but also as a way to test the area of the man that most brings her anxiety. This is why a man should expect pushback when he explains sexual polarity and masculine frame to his woman. He must realize that a woman is designed to play devil's advocate to his viewpoint but also must realize that our species has two worldviews. There is a masculine worldview that is based on rationale and a feminine worldview based on emotion. The worldview itself divides the sexes and keeps them from absolute agreement over reality. It is like someone with sight is explaining what he sees to someone without sight. The one without vision who exists in the dark of himself will be like the female who bases her perspective on how she feels in the environment. The eye is detached from the rest of our senses just as rationale is detached from the emotional underlining. What does it mean to only see with our eyes and not be able to feel with our body or to hear with our ears? This is the core trouble with the sexes sharing the same worldview. But there is something deeper to why a woman will never truly be able to articulate the sexual polarity that most gives her pleasure. She understands it when it is upon her but she will not know the means of production that brings about the result. The core reason is a woman is psychologically teased by how the masculine frame holds back what she most desires. It is in the restraint and measured out fruits of desire that most entrances a female into the possession of a man's frame. When a man holds back what a woman most desires, she desires it more so. But if we were to ask a female what she most wants in a man, she will say that she does not want a man to hold back her from her desires but rather readily give into her wants. It is the overabundance of her desires being fulfilled that most destroys her own passions.

A man know that he holds back and teases a female to excite her into attachment. He knows that a woman will never admit that this is his means to production. She does not want to know how the sausage is made, she just wants to enjoy it when it is upon her. But when a man reveals the truth of female arousal to a woman, she will disagree fundamentally because she does not want to feel gamed like an animal into expected behaviorism. The rationale worldview is cold. A man does not need to have emotion for a female to make her have emotion for him. He merely needs to understand how to behave in masculine restraint around her and project power to spike emotional attachment in her. The cold explanation itself dispels the warm emotion that was built with imaginative detail inside the woman's mind. It is like a joke losing its humor when it needs to be explained. Once something is broken apart in explanation, it loses the impact of its emotional effect from when it was previous whole. But even if a woman does agree with a man in the moment about polarity and frame, she will disagree with him when her emotional state changes. A woman can build whatever narrative she needs to ease her anxiety and to calm her emotion. This is the reason why a woman can fall into Stockholm syndrome. The narrative we build is how we protect our emotional view of the reality we exist inside. We will create the grandest lies to protect ourselves from the darkest despairs. If knowing how the sausage is made in romance robs a woman of her sexual appetite, she will will herself into amnesia over its production. Since a woman is dual in her nature and psychology, she can easily think about all things being subjective in meaning which allows her to create the necessary illusions to protect her worldview.

A woman does not fall into love with a man's explanation, she falls in love with his presentation. The tone is set by the male and not the female. Masculinity creates femininity. It is up to the man to lead sexual polarity by being above the confused leadership of the female. She would destroy her own sexual desire if she led the man to her passions. A man must be above the doubt and challenges to how he creates the needed illusion for them both to exist inside. The man's frame in its masculine restraint draws the woman's desire towards him. He keeps her craving more. He keeps her chasing his affection. He keeps what she most desires just out of her reach and she will never admit that this is the key to her heart.

All women seek power over men from anxiety

When we feel helpless in an environment, we will feel anxiety from that lack of control. The key reason why men and women both battle anxiety issues is due to a feeling of helplessness. If a man depends on others for his own salvation, he will be anxious in their arrival and success. This feeling of paralysis causes us to exist in a state of internal conflict from the dependency we place on others to solve our problems. Men who truly take to heart the core of my philosophy of "to be a man is to bear the responsibility of all things", free themselves of the heavy anxiety of that dependency of passivity. To be responsible is to be responsive. We take responsibility for our lives by actively responding to how we fit into the world that surrounds us. This requires action. This requires us to *impress our will* on our environment. We are either waiting for salvation or we are acting as savior. The more anxious state is the position of waiting for salvation. This is the fundamental reason why women are more anxious creatures than men. Their own passivity in sexual selection creates high anxiety in that act of waiting. Their dependency on a man fulfilling their burden of performance and leading them in selection causes them to have internal conflict which creates neurotic disorder. Since females are reliant on males in sexual selection, this causes them to blame and complain about males in our selection. This is all part of a female's animal design. To blame and complain is to vent impotence in power to the will of another. The more we complain and blame others for our lives, the less authority we give ourselves in our lives.

When a woman complains about her man, she is complaining about failed expectations in his authority over her. She vents to her social circle as a way to regulate her emotional state within a state of helplessness. The act of talking is a false action that mitigates the anxiety but builds connections of empathy within feminine collectives. The drama of indignation incites the group based on the relationship trouble of a part of the sisterhood. But what a man must realize is the anxiety is the precursor of intelligence. We must worry about a problem before we solve it. This is why the most intellectually dense humans on the planet are the most carefree. And why intelligence and neuroticism usually corelate. The more we feel helpless in an environment the more we feel imprisoned to our body within it. From this state of body paralysis, we become confined to the mind. This is why we usually see a "man of action" as less intelligent as the man who has trained himself to intellectualize his cowardice. When we cannot rely on brute strength, we must rely on our sense of wits.

Women hold a tremendous gift of wit in social manipulations that creates great authority in power dynamics but becomes hampered by their own biological design. A woman is her own worst enemy and a major reason why females consistently divide amongst themselves. Place a group of women together in a room and there will be division right down the middle. A woman is dual in nature which means she wars against herself. So even though a woman is groomed for strong wit by her passivity, she is restricted in the totality of her power potential from her own psychological confusion. The majority of women are more knowing of human nature and of power dynamics than the men they are in relationships with. This state of knowing causes them tremendous anxiety as they feel their authority is sounder than the authority of their males. A reason why women seek out "bad boys," is because these types of men project a more solid knowing of the power dynamics of the world. They exist above the game that others do not know they are playing and therefore gain advantage from that knowledge. Women easily fall into a mother/son dynamic with their men because they are conditioned to understand power dynamics more than the average male. Why? Because a woman's genitalia out of sight makes her entire body become an erogenous zone to her sexual stimulation and the mystery of her sex organs places her in body paralysis needed for inward introspection based on that stimulation. And what most stimulates a female's body in her selection? Power. This means that a female becomes highly attuned to the shifts of power in an environment because her body purrs when she finds sexual attraction based on the power projection.

All women are "power detectives" because the mystery of power leads them back to their sexual pleasure. What this means is that women have an advantage of psychology over the majority of males because of this sensitivity to power dynamics. The anxiety turns to arousal and makes them attune themselves in search of the arousal of power that could calm that anxiety. The innate anxiety a woman feels and the greater capacity for knowing power dynamics compels her to solve her anxiety by taking control of her man in a relationship. The anxiety women feel overwhelms them and causes them to break free of the passivity of their selection to lead their men. But the control they get over their men is a defective solution to their anxiety. A woman needs a masculine leader in her selection because of her reproductive fear in carrying the man's child and being confined to the nest to nurture his children. She desires a man who is more knowing than her because she must rely on the man as the figure who gets resource from the world outside the nest and who protects the nest from the world. This is why a woman seeks an experienced man in sexual selection, she desires a man who is not afraid to explore because it means he will carry a greater knowledge of human nature and the world itself.

The reason why men seek out less experienced females is that we innately know that a woman must satisfy herself to the confinement of the nest and not feel that she is missing out on the worldly pleasures she has grown accustomed from previous experience. We do not miss what we have not known. A reason why two people who are sexually inexperienced are able to manage the loyalty of a long-term monogamous commitment. When a woman is more knowing of man in terms of power dynamics, she will more easily assume authority over him. But since she unconsciously knows of the biological burden of pregnancy and the irrationality of her body's design, she will carry resentment in the authority she gained over her man. Think about it like this. A woman is a passenger in a car and the male is in the driver seat. The male is goofing off and not paying attention to the road ahead of them. He is distracted and the car veers in and out of the lanes. There is oncoming traffic and the cars swerve to avoid them. How would this make the passenger feel? She would hold high anxiety in her helplessness from the dependency she holds on the irresponsible driver. Her reliance on him and his failure in driving them both will make her an anxious mess. She will test him. She will point ahead and try to help him drive. This is the basic design of female "nagging" and testing. It is an expression of anxiety from failed leadership. But after much help to the irresponsible male driver, the woman will feel compelled to take the wheel and drive them both. This is how a mother/son dynamic forms in a relationship. She will then hold tremendous resentment and bitterness over the failed driving of the male. Why? Because she innately knows that she is not designed for driving them both. She knows that the man is designed for driving and that she is subverting both their design. Her anxiety now is not solved but rather skyrockets. Why? Because she now must imagine herself driving while caring for an infant. "How am I going to manage to devote myself to the helplessness of an infant and its anxiety to a world that makes it dependent on the mother to ease that anxiety when the mother herself is burdened with not only nurturing within the nest but also protecting/providing for the nest?" The woman looks over to the male who is blissfully looking at the scenery like a daydreaming child.

"Damn him" she curses to herself. This is why the more control a female gets over a male the more she will grow to despise him in her heart. If a woman is to play the role of female by carrying a child in womb, the man must also play his role. The female protects the child in her womb and later in her arms while the male protects them both. When a woman is forced into a position where she must not only care for herself but also a male who is derelict in his duty, she will lose all attraction to him and feel finding a new mate as a matter of survival. And she is right to think that. This is what a man cucks himself. A woman cheats on a male when the male fails her. It is the male's responsibility to lead a woman and to protect/provide for her. Remember, regardless if a male or a female has a child together, the inherent programming will always be there. The hidden algorithm of procreate influences all human behavior regardless if it sought in intention.

Equality is a lie to transfer power

The core design of a female is to either dominate a male or to submit to him in our sexual selection. A female is designed to test a man's sense of authority and will become emboldened over him the more the male fails the tests. Think about it like this. A woman is designed to dominate a male but is reassured when a male does not allow her to dominate him. The mating dance of our species is a woman trying to get power over a male and having her reproductive anxiety calmed when the male refuses to give her control. If the male fails the test, this signals to the female that she needs to take charge in the relationship which creates resentment over that power transfer since she is in need of a sexual leader from her biological investment in pregnancy.

A woman is always reaching for power because of her high sex anxiety from her biological imperative to carry the male's offspring. The extreme body transformation of female pregnancy causes a woman to always test power configurations in her environment. Most males are oblivious to the power structures that surround them but women are highly attune to the social power structure. They use this intuition as a way for mate decisioning in their selection. They understand the most subtle expressions of power in social situations. They are power obsessed by design to select males for propagation and to reassure themselves of that decision. But a woman's main test in male authority is psychological warfare and not physical. She misdirects, gaslights and uses subterfuge to test male authority. This is a major reason why women sexual reward men who are "bad boys." These men play by their own rules and are not beholden to the will of others. Their selfishness represents a singular vision that cuts through the testing of female tactics. But also, their selfishness creates an indifference which causes them to be above the direction and will of others. The less shame and guilt tactics work on a man, the more aroused in indignation a female will be by his rebellious nature. The greatest act of mind games and gaslighting is to make someone think they are something that they are not. For example, a woman is designed to seek power over a male and to be reassured by his authority. She is hyper sensitive to power dynamics in all social dynamics. *But she will make a male think he is power obsessed when he does not submit to her will.* If the male feels shame over his "power obsession", he will then be compelled to stop seeking it. This is similar to convincing an opponent in war to set down their weapons while staying armed.

Women as the physically weaker sex have had to rely on wits to transfer power from males to them. This is a reason why women moralize emotion and work to make modern man sensitive in emotion. Once a male is sensitive in emotion, he can be sensitive to emotional control. But while a female is power obsessed, she will honestly deny this. All female psychology is dual in nature. A woman is both power obsessed and ignorant of power. Think about it like this. A woman will have a cold calculation for her behavior but will then sweep the logical footsteps away that led her there by emotionally gaslighting herself. This is why a female can have a cold burden of performance in sexual selection but then after she falls "in love" with a male, she will forget all about that initial cold conditional view of romance. She wills herself to forget what she finds shameful to her sense of identity. There is a natural contradiction to female psychology which is why women hold high irrationality. What a man must realize is that all power in this world is either gained by fraud of force. We either show people the truth of our strength or we make them think we are stronger than we truly are. Since females are physically weaker than males, they must rely on fraud to gain control over them. How does a female control a male in a romantic relationship? She controls through guilt and shame tactics. How do feminists control men in our societies? They control by with guilt and shame tactics. They emotionally gaslight men into submission. They make males feel noble in letting down their guard as "big men" as they assume authority over them. Remember, there is not a place on earth that is free of power structure. There is no magical place in human reality where there is a vacuum of power. We are either leading others or being led by others. *Equality is a lie to transfer power*. Equality in power is gaslight for control. There is no equality of power in nature. There is only give and take. There is only a struggle for power and a triumph of will. This is true of lions and gazelles in the grasslands of Africa and this is true of the relationship between males and females. We are in constant conflict and struggle as a living organism. We are liberated from power only in death.

Once a man understands that females seek power by emotional manipulation, his eyes will be opened to this political world. Feminists have both with one hand demonized males as power obsessed while holding in the other hand radical ideology about redistribution of current power systems. Ask a radical feminist what constitutes a "racist" and she will not just say that is means when someone hates someone of a different race but rather when *someone who holds power* hates someone of a different race. All modern feminist ideology is laced with power obsessions and guilt systems to attain that power. This is why we see women in our times using a multitude of shame labels to silence opposition and to guilt submission in their opponents. A man can be called all kinds of "-phobe" labels or he can be called a sexist or he can be called a racist. Social shame and group pressure is how females' control. They use social reputation as their weapon of choice. Why? Because it is their own greatest fear and so they turn it on others. Women fear being outcast from their peer groups more than anything else. They hold deep anxiety over being singled out for social shame. When a man no longer can be controlled over shame labels, he becomes someone who cannot be controlled by women. Who cares if someone thinks a man is racist? Or sexist? Or some kind of "-phobe?" The label only works to control when it gets an emotional reaction.

Once a man knows the psychological game of power that women play, he can choose to quit that game and play his own. There is a massive demonization of "white straight men" in our times by radical feminists. Why? The simplest reason is that white males have gotten weak to emotional control and their wives and daughters have become emboldened over them. They attack weakness even if it is in their own house. What happens if a man becomes weak in a relationship with a woman? She will begin to test him in public and try to emasculate him before others. This is her animal nature. And this is the reason why white women are openly mocking their white fathers.

I was raised Christian and believe that people can live in harmony if they have shared religious belief regardless of skin color. But the behaviorism of modern women is simplistic in its design and they are trying to gaslight men into submission. All races on earth have either committed war or enslaved others. There was war in Africa before whites showed up. Native Americans where waging territorial warfare before whites showed up. All human beings have been in a struggle for power and have exploited each other. No one is free of sin on this planet. Nations are either forcing their will on others are frauding others to surrender their will without a fight. The only reason why there is a "white guilt" in our times is to transfer power. It is just another form of feminine tactics for control by emotional shaming. A woman obsessively keeps track of past trauma in arguments in a relationship and when women rule the world, the history of past trauma of nations becomes eternal in obsession. Only men can let go of the past. Only men let grudges die. But in a world ran by women, our victim stories get us power. This is the reason why there is a growing cult of victimhood that is infecting our reality. This is why people are choosing to be marginalized as sexual eccentrics so that they can get their precious victim story. This is why people are reaching back hundreds of years for victimhood. It is all a way to transfer power in a feminine time period. It is power obsession. And when this generation of men free themselves of emotional sensitivity, they will be free of emotional control. Then they will march into a future where the past does not hold them back. They will not have to bear the trauma of their ancestors and they will not have to bear the guilt of their forefathers. That is a future I believe in. Join me.

Ignorant of the means of production

The capacity for greatness in mankind is due to obsession, drive and humility. A man must be obsessed in singular focus on pursuing his passion, he must have the energy to pursue it and he must adapt himself for success. Worldly ambition is a redirect of sexual ambition. Men have a fundamental problem of sexual access that most forms them when they are in the sexual heat of young manhood. They want sex and must figure out how to get it. They form themselves to the burden of performance that females place on them in our sexual selection. They either form their body in muscle to display themselves as protector or they hustle in career ambition to set themselves up as provider. The formation of male ambition is fundamentally a problem of procreation. Whether a man says he does all this for himself alone, it is ignorance of the unconscious drive that motivates his behaviorism. A man will invest tremendous energy in his ambition for either a conscious or unconscious pay off of reproductive privilege. This is the core means of production not just in a man's individual behavior but in the behaviorism of males across our world. *The means of production in sex is the means of production in all things*. But even when a man consciously starts his own personal ambition as a way for sexual access, he will sometimes fall in love with the pursuit more than the original objective. This how we get the true greats among human history. These men started the ambition as a means for either conscious or unconscious sex but soon fall into obsession over the ambition more than the prospect of sex. They enjoyed the journey so much that they forgot the destination and kept traveling. When a man becomes obsessed over his ambition, he will place it above all his most basic needs and desires. It becomes his ultimate desire and brings him the most satisfaction. This is true of Mozart, Nietzsche, Einstein and all genius obsessives. The journey of personal ambition was started as a solution to a problem of sex and the destination becomes forsaken for a furthering of the journey itself. But it is the female's burden of performance in our selection which conditions males for greatness.

When a female places a varied criteria of expectation of a male in sex, she is ultimately telling him that he is either worthy or unworthy of reproductive privilege. A lot of men think that male superiority comes from a biological reason which ignores the greater psychological influence that the female places on the male in our selection. But it is not just the burden of performance that creates male superiority but rather the amount of rejection that men experience in our selection that grooms them in the humility needed for greatness. To be great requires not just the ego to impress our will on the world but also humility in allowing the world to shape us. This can be perfectly illustrated by a male who wants success with women. He must feel himself worthy enough to make attempt of his desires by approaching a female while at the same time accepting a female's rejection as a personal failure on his own part. It is a mixture of ego and humility. We must summon a sense of worth enough for making attempts while allowing our sense of self to be shaped by a truth outside ourself. For example, a man must be brave enough to enter a cave that holds grand treasure but humble enough to lower his head to enter the cave's mouth. Higher consciousness is a fancy way of saying super adaptation. The capacity to learn from failure is how our species is able to adapt to the world that seeks to destroy us. Insanity is in doing the same thing over and over while expecting a different result. We show sanity when we reconfigure our attempts in failure. Sanity is growth while insanity is stagnation that leads to decay. When a man learns to be good with women, he must sacrifice his preconceived view of how women should be and lets the reality humble him. He must overcome himself to be something greater in the world. He must summon a drive in the world to solve his sexual problem. He is not allowed to act as an egg carrying nester and merely present himself for approach but rather make brave attempt at risk of failure. A man must risk the humiliation of rejection which humbles his ego and allows him the necessary emotional detachment for repeated trial. It is not merely a stabilized hormone in the body or testosterone that creates male superiority but rather the burden of performance placed on males that forces them into superiority. The vast number of services and goods that our civilization produces is based on not just the necessity for life but rather the imperative to sex. The greatest human achievements in our species have been due to the runaway sexual ambition of a few males.

Female mediocrity is not from hormone flux or a lack of testosterone but rather lack of sexual desperation that fuels ingenuity. Albert Einstein once said "Necessity is the mother of all invention"—Men must invent novel approaches in their sexual selection and that psychology informs their capacity for invention in our reality. The fundamental motivation behind the means of production in our species is the compelled necessity of sex anxiety. Men make money to get sexual access to women while women make money to be free of undesirable providers who want sexual access. The struggle that is inherent to male sexual selection creates the suffering needed for not only personal development but in the development of our species.

A woman does not want to know what it truly requires for a man to fulfil his burden of performance of her, she wants him to perform it. She does not want to see him grinding, she merely wants him to display the sharpness of his blade. A woman may be aroused by a man's muscular body but she will be repulsed by having to witness how many hours he spends in the gym and the preciousness of his calorie counting. The source of power behind the curtain of mystery is what dispels a woman of her aroused curiosity. Most playboy men only become playboys from countless experiences of rejections upon rejections and failures upon failures. A woman may be aroused by the smoothness of a playboy but would immediately lose attraction if she understood the learning experience of what it takes to become a playboy. This is a fundamental ignorance of the means of production. She wants the end product, she does not want to see how much work went into its creation. This is true of all things in a woman's worldview. She wants things to appear at her doorstep ready to go. This end point focus on production is inherent to her own innate arrival at her sexual value. A woman is born with sexual value and grows into it. She does not have to figure out a complicated burden of performance from males to fulfil. She does not need to fail, fail, fail and be rejected to learn how to get sex. No. She merely needs to present and submit. This fundamental laziness in sexual selection is the reason why women achieve fewer great works than men. It is not a hormone issue. It is not due to a male sex drive. It is due to the very fact that men must humble themselves in adaptation to the female's steep burden of performance. But more specifically why women entering the work force has not provided female greatness. It is due to that lack of necessity in their sexual selection. A woman does not need to pursue worldly ambition to solve her sexual problem like a man. Her ambition is driven to a self-sufficiency enough to be free of inferior providers. It is a bare minimum effort for financial liberation. Women are fundamentally mediocre in ambition because they lack a steep burden of performance placed upon them like males. The means of production is limited to what is minimally sufficient for survival among females because it is not based on attaining sexual access but rather being freed from it. Feminist are confused when they think that their career ambitions can be equally matched to men. They deny the root cause of a male's ambition and therefore become ignorant over what it requires to match the production. A woman who makes money becomes a "strong and independent" whereas a man who makes money becomes a provider for not only a female as dependent but also any children they have together. This fundamental difference causes a male to focus his power beyond himself and not be confined to himself. A reason why a male becomes superior to a female while a female remains in a state of mediocrity.

It is common among females to hate free enterprise and to support systems of collective support. These systems of collective support usually at the foundation are about taking care of people's base needs whether housing, food or medical. A man will notice that radical feminism is about redistribution of wealth and governmental provisioning over a citizenry's necessities. But once a man's eyes open to the truth of the female animal, he will see through all their political desires as a solution to their sex anxieties. For example, a female is an egg carrying nester who wants to nest while another provides for her. She wants to be housed, fed and provided for while she cares for children. When women wanted to join a system of free enterprise, they happily joined as a way to free themselves of the dependency to genetically inferior provider males. But once enough females become "strong and independent" in a system of free enterprise, they will try to destroy the system because it further shows their incompetency within it. Males are designed for worldly ambition and produce resource as a way to support females who are nesting while females support themselves alone only so they can be free of undesirable men. The system of free enterprise aligns with males more than females only because it aligns with the burden of performance that females place on males. A career man is sexually desirable to women while a career woman is not desirable to men. Women politically fought to enter the power hierarchy of men only to realize that they do not sexual benefit from ascension within that hierarchy.

When a man rises in power and wealth, his sexual opportunities widen while a woman who rises in power and wealth will see her sexual opportunities dry up. The more females realize that they joined a game that mostly benefits males, the more they will want to not only quit the game but rather prove the game must be destroyed in order to save face. When they destroy the game that most benefits the sexual strategy of men, they will castrate the means of production that comes from the male sexual strategy. For example, when a female sets up a system where basic needs are provided to an entire population, the fundamental problem of how to motivate a work force to produce goods arises. The majority of males are not motivated beyond necessity. The base provider role of males is to make a primitive nest for females and to support them for survival. Only a few males are motivated by luxury and not necessity. Men will wake up and go to work so that they can house and feed their families. When that foundational need no longer motivates them, they choose not to work. This is why a collectivist system where basic needs are provided to the masses eventually decays from the base motivation of survival being satisfied which *denies the means of production for that society.*

The well-meaning but ignorant collective eventually turns violent as the satisfied residents soon must be motivated beyond basic means of survival. They are motivated by individual fear of death instead of individual fear of homelessness. Once a man realizes my philosophy, he will begin to see that there will be a growing sentiment to destroy a system of free enterprise only because females have grown tired of competing within it. But even further in the innate ignorance that women have about the means of production is in the ignorance of how wealth accumulates. The rich get richer and the poor get richer because of the sexual selection of females. Why? All a system of material wealth is based on the undercurrent system of sexual access. Men seek wealth and power only because these allow them access to the most beautiful and fertile women. But how does wealth and power accumulate? Social proof.

Why do women become more aroused by a man who is already being pursued by women? This is the key to understand unfair distribution of power and wealth. A woman will pursue a man who is already in sexual abundance because he represents a low risk to her reproductive anxiety. The safer the bet, the less need for critical thought. This is why the masses will fall into imitation of a few trendsetters among them. This is why a restaurant that has a line out front will get more business while an empty restaurant will further spiral into desperation. Abundance breeds abundance while desperation breeds further desperation. *The poor create the rich, the rich do not create the poor.* When a female falls into competition with other females for the attention of a single man, she becomes the reason why there is an unequal distribution of wealth in civilization. Feminists who want to redistribute wealth are wanting to redistribute the fruits of a means of production that their own sexual behavior has influenced. They want to equally distribute the fruits of a tree while ignoring what waters the tree itself. This innate myopic foolishness is why men have been assigned headship positions in all the major religions and why a male dominated patriarchy not only exists but thrives. When women get power, they ignore how the source of the power was achieved and it withers in their hands.

A forbidden fruit above heads

Power can either be gained by fraud or force. We can either inspire submission or force it upon others. Why would inspiration be fraudulent? Because a leader must project more strength than what he truly has inside him. He must hide his weakness and project strength. When a man carries strong frame, others will think him much stronger than he thinks himself. People follow not strength in truth but rather their own imaginations. This is true of all human interactions, but especially women, since they base their sexual pleasure on it. Is it truly a lie if a man is showing only strength and hiding his weaknesses? It is an exaggeration of truth that creates a fraudulent embellishment.

The best stories are told with a flare of exaggeration. Legends and myths grow not from the bare truth laid out in autistic detail but rather in the shared emotional connection with figures and events. Our shared emotional imagination is what we carry forward through thousands of years and not the dry bones of reality. They are long buried and forgotten for the roaming ghosts of fantasy. What a man must realize about the sexes of our species is that we are in an eternal conflict for supremacy and have battled over gaining power over each other for millennia upon millennia. A physically small female is either emotional manipulating a giant brute of a male or a slubby male is tricking a beautiful female into loving him. When a man carries strong masculine frame, he is projecting an exaggerated strength that reassures a woman's reproductive anxiety which allows her to form emotional attachment and fall into a contented submission to his authority. When a man shrugs frame, a woman will try to seize control over him with emotional or sexual manipulations as a way to gain power over him so that she can ease her own reproductive anxiety. Both sides are in a constant struggle for power which is based on each attempting to solve their own sex anxieties. A woman will act as nurturer to a man in a relationship as a way to incite his emotionalism. It could be through the warmth of touch or the thoughtfulness of gift giving. What she is doing is trying to get the man to let his guard down and build an emotional dependency on her. Mothers do this to their children and women do this to men in relationships. The more a man has an emotional dependency on a female, the more he allows himself to be emotionally controlled by her. It starts with building an emotional attachment which is a psychological reminiscence of son to mother which creates the feminine frame of authority. A woman will purposely act as emotional comforter to her man as an act of intimacy which creates his dependency on her. Once he is in her hands, she will be able to manipulate him with ease. This is why men who openly talk about using their females for emotional comfort are the same males who most susceptible to guilt and same tactics. A woman will utilize that same emotional sensitivity she has nurtured for attachment as a means of power later on. This is why a giant beast of a man can still be ruled at home by his female. His emotional weakness places him into a place of submission to the feminine frame of authority. The key problem to the male is that he wants something that he should not have. He wants to reexperience the love his mother or the love of a mother he never had. He wants to remain in a prison of sentimentality and so he sacrifices the future for a reimagined past. The illusion is that he moralizes emotion which makes him play by the rules in a woman's game. The smaller, more vulnerable and more nurturing a female behaves with a man, the more he perceives her as purely good in her intentions which creates a mother image in his mind. But he does not realize that unconditional love is only for mothers and their children.

There is a cold calculation to the conditions of romance that creates the burden of performance that the man unwittingly follows as he imagines an unconditional love pouring out from his woman's nurture. The giant male who is submissive to his female will view her as pure and moral in angelic fantasy. He overlooks the struggle for power because he wants to lower his guard in blind trust to the will of another. Believing a woman is above the struggle for power is the grandest illusion that men hold inside themselves. When we can trust authority as having our absolute best interests in heart allows us to fall into a blissful obedience without critical worry. When the power above is holy, we bathe in ignorance to the surrender of our will to it. This is what headship means. Our head does the thinking and the body can submit to its will. A man who no longer has to worry about power dynamics is either ignorant or dead. It is willful ignorance that compels beast of men to surrender themselves into feminine authority. They want to believe women are not power hungry for control over them based on selfish reasons because they want to justify the surrender of the power in order to relax their guard. Just as a whisper into a night watchman's ear of sleep will soon lure him into tragedy, the same for a man who allows the siren song of female authority lure him out of his masculine frame. Once the power shifts from male to female, the female will then attack the male because he failed her ultimate test. What she thought would solve her sex anxiety only doubled it. This is why weak men create Jezebels. The transfer of power from a man to a woman is a devil's bargain. It will soon consume the man and emasculate him in entirety. He will have wished that he stayed vigilant on watch to invading forces who surrounded the outer wall of his kingdom.

We all want what is just out of our reach but close enough to lure us to it. Women will call men "power mad" but will climb over each other in sexual competition for powerful men. What this generation of men must realize about women is that they are eternally discontent which means they are eternally grasping things beyond their reach and become disenchanted by things finally held in hand. How can a man be good with women from the start? He must project that he is superior to them and project confidence in his authority with masculine frame. This is all power projection. Women see power like a shiny diamond of enchantment that must be pursued and followed. Who was most tempted by the forbidden fruit in the garden of Eden? It was the woman. Why? Adam had no use for more power since he was sexually satisfied with Eve but Eve was dissatisfied with her place in power. She wanted to be like God in his knowledge. She wanted to share *the knowing* of one who is in power. Why do women like bad boys? These men showcase a strong understanding of human nature and are more *knowing* than women. A woman seeks out a powerful man because it is the man's power that most eases her reproductive anxiety. She wants to give birth to his children because that power will grow within her. When a man acts with indifference and ego in sexual selection, it acts as a strong lure to women. Women like arrogant men who are "cocky" because these men embellish their own power source. And women fall victim to the embellishment of power just as men fall victim to the moralization of emotion. And just like that we all fall victim to enjoying an embellished story, we know to be false. Both our exaggerations of the truth of reality. Both are frauds to gain power over another. But we do not blame a good salesman who sells us something we do not need. We blame ourselves for being naïve to exploitations. This is the same for women and playboys in sex. These types of men embellish themselves with sweet lies to gain sexual access and women blame themselves for falling victim to their charms.

When a man showcases a pride in his sexual value, he is inflating a price that a woman is willing to pay. We all like good deals and we do not want to lose out on getting them. This is based on a fear of loss. A man who projects power with his frame, will ease a woman's sex anxiety and creates a tremendous fear of loss over losing the power source. And it is from that fear of loss that a woman will make concessions in negotiations that transfers power from her to the man. She does not want to lose the power that eases her anxiety just as a man who is under the frame of authority of his woman does not want to lose the emotional comfort of her authority over him. The fear of loss in a woman's heart for the distant power that her man holds will keep her chasing him. Women who chase affection are too busy to be bored. And boredom is what creates the curiosity that leads to the exit from Eden.

While both sexes struggle for power in a relationship, only the male can hold power over the female without resentment or bitterness. This is why relationships strengthen based on male authority and female submission. A woman will seek power over a man but she will resent it as soon as it falls into her hands. She most craves what is just out of reach. This is why a man who cannot be emotionally controlled not only frees himself of feminine authority by ends up satisfying his female who is looking for a sense of independence in her man. She wants to submit to a man who is not easily lured away from his defenses. She wants a man who understands that she is not innocent to power. She wants a man who is outside her control and just out of her reach.

A falling tree in the dark

The myopic emotional worldview of easy indulgence and impulsivity is the final days of a dying world. When women hold too much power over the psychological upbringing of children, the feminine frame behaviorism begins to accelerate. Easy divorce that has led to single mother culture is the reason why we are spiraling into decay. A woman is a momentary creature who is not meant to plan for the future. She is meant for vulnerable attentiveness to the care of children. Her shortsightedness is by design to allow her the close focus for nurturing. Her emotional sensitivity is meant to be protected by a man's cold frame so as to allow her the needed empathy for caring for the helplessness of human infancy. The females of our species are symbolic of darkness. Remember, a man is objective in his focus from biological certainty over his sex organ in its singularity and his rationality is sharpened by the necessity for problem solving over the sexual burden that females place on him in our selection. A man must learn from his past mistakes in repeated rejection in selection which means he must humbly submit himself to the value of history. He holds in his hand the preservation of tradition and in the other futurism of possible outcomes. One foot in the past and one foot in the future. The female metaphorically nests between his legs as a human symbol for the here and now. She is under his frame and her feminine submission grounds him to the moment.

When a civilization is in its feminine frame, it falls into a perpetual moment or a "living for the day." There is no respect for tradition and history. There is no thought or preparation for the future. Both legs of the symbolic male frame have been cut out from under him like in Daniels prophecy. Only the shortsighted pursuit of temporary pleasure satisfies this dying world. The world has fallen to its knees because it has only stood on the symbolic legs of man (past/future). Men have fallen and women have arisen to power only because of that failure of mankind.

Women are not to blame. Remember, a female is designed to test a male's authority in our selection as a way to calm her reproductive anxiety and to challenge the man to betterment. But when a male allows his female to dominate him, she will then become cruel in being exposed to the world outside his frame. She will then attack him in high resentment and bitterness. This is the state of womankind in a world where men have abandoned their frames for the comfort of motherly illusions. They hide themselves away in sexual desperations and emotional dependencies while women rule the world. And this world will reflect the heart of womankind. A resentful and bitter heart of dominance over mankind. An unchecked obsession with openness that destroys meaning. The male's psychology is symbolic of objectivity while the female is symbolic of subjectivity. Remember, she is in the dark about her sex organ, she relies on a finely attuned intuition from feeling her way through reality and that blindless towards herself makes her subjective in perception towards reality. The hormone flux that creates the duality in temperament creates an irrationality that creates an anxiety that is calmed only by the acceptance of two truths. This split perception makes a woman war against objective truth only because it reveals the two headed dragon in her own mind. Objective meaning is an ugly mirror that she refuses to look upon. It is the man's job to face the objective world. When women get power over the world, the world will begin to become more subjective in meanings which means it decays from the dissolution of definitions. Certainty is confidence, and confidence is needed to navigate a world seeking to destroy us. Subjectivity is doubt and this doubt allows a world seeking to destroy us to overwhelm our defenses. An imitation of a female body letting down her guard from belief in the power of the other and her wet acceptance of surrender. The obsession with open acceptance of all things like open legs and open gates to a bodily kingdom.

What a man must realize about what hyper feminization means is that it is an unabashed warring against traditional norms by design that have anchored peoples to the earth and it is a breakdown of meaning not just in words and sex, but all things. It is a blindness that is spreading across the earth and is causing mass confusion. A darkness is spreading over this world and it comes from the heart of a woman. The human eye allows us to narrow our mind to what can be seen. Without our eyes, the rest of our senses open up in unlimited interpretations over the uncertainty of the surrounding world. Man has been assigned as head over the woman in religious scripture not just because the man's frame must be outside the woman to calm her reproductive anxiety but because the man is a symbol of forethought, far sightedness and clear vision. Just as emotions cloud critical judgment, the emotional worldview is blind to reality.

In Jeremiah 17:9 it says "The heart is more deceitful than all else And is desperately sick; Who can understand it?" The head should lead the heart, not the reverse. Women lead with short sighted compassion without understanding the far-reaching consequences of their compassions. They are blind feelers to reality meant for nurturing in the nest where their heightened feel can bring warmth to offspring. Just as a female in nest with children can be indulgent to their needs, she will be ignorant of the discipline needed to lead them to greater independence from her. This is why the one outside the nest, the male, is the one who must teach the offspring that the nest experience is temporary and so he disciplines with a view of that eventual departure. When women rule the world, they will apply the undisciplined indulgence of "just be yourself" and "born this way" as ways for further infantilization. It is a mock imitation of a mother over child who indulges to counterbalance the masculine discipline of becoming over being. The "fat acceptance", proliferation of drug culture and homosexual celebrations in our times are symptoms of the irrationality of forsaking tomorrow for today. It is shortsightedness based on emotional reasoning that will eventually lead to a hard awakening when things start to fall apart. And then this world will realize what it means for the blind to lead the blind. They will understand what it means to charge blindly into ill prepared future. It will be like children who resent their mother's love only because that love built a dependency on her and did not prepare them for a world seeking to destroy them.

It is a mother's role to nurture her offspring to make them feel loved and it is a father's role to discipline his children with high expectations to prepare them for life outside the nest. With the rise of fatherlessness, we are not being prepared for our future. The world is ending because nobody wants to carry it forward. This final generation have been nurtured in a nest on a falling tree. Once the tree falls, their wings will be too weak to fly away from the collapse. We must shine our light on the world. We must open our eyes to the reality before us. We must discipline ourselves and give defined meaning to his world. We must protect boundaries, borders and definitions. We must protect tradition and history from those seeking to destroy it. We must pass frame each man to the next. A generation of orphans must become the fathers they never had. We must teach each other how to fly before the tree falls.

Protection against men

When females get dominance over males, they will hold greater reproductive anxiety. The reason is that a female is designed to submit herself to a man who views as a protector/provider. Women who become dominants over their males in relationships will have high reproductive anxiety. They will not want to bear the offspring of their males and will abandon their own sexual burden. What is a female's sexual burden? It is a complimentary nature with a physically healthy body which is neither overly thin or overly fat. The hourglass form is one of fertility. While a male has a steep burden of performance that he must bear, a woman has a much smaller burden of performance that she bears for sexual selection. She must humble herself to the male gaze as a way to appeal to men. When women gain power in a civilization, they will begin to gain fat on their bodies in rebellion to the male gaze. From their dominance, they will both hold a high reproductive anxiety while dismissing their own burden of performance from arrogance in their selection.

It is not a coincidence that the "fat acceptance" movement has become the norm of our times where women have gained more and more control over men. Just as a man cannot decide the criteria for the burden of performance that females place on him, a female cannot define what men view as beauty. She either submits to the male gaze's definition or she rebels against that definition. And the reason why she would rebel against the narrow definition of the male gaze is because it requires humility from her place of power.

The biggest taboo in our times is women submitting to the desires and authority of men. The female liberation movement is freedom from the subjugation of male control. Females being unattractive is a shit test to the small burden of performance that males place on them. This is why there is a rise of obesity along with a celebration of "queer aesthetic." This can be seen among hipster feminists who purposely make bad fashion choices with a sense of irony as way to make what is ugly chic. They playfully shit test the disciplined sense of beauty that has come from the male gaze. They will wear mismatched muddy colors in purposeful ugliness. Their clothes will be tight across their unattractive bodies in mock confidence as they sell humor in all seriousness. The overabundance of irony is a symptom of hyper feminization as this generation can have an intellectual detachment to their own passivity and decay. The fat hipster girl is the embodiment of queer aesthetic run amok. The refashioning of style is witchcraft manifest over substance. The style is just not based on the attractiveness of the designs but rather the over confidence in selling the ugliness. All the most famous art by these obese feminists represents the breakdown of masculine discipline as what is primitive, even to child standards, is placed in art galleries as collective belief in nonsense. A fat and sloppy female will wrap herself tight in kitschy flare as the symbol of rebellion to the male gaze. Her proud ugliness to the male standards of beauty is like a belly loosened from a tight belt. She sighs in relief to her freedom from not just male gaze but also the possibility of where the gaze leads. This is what a man must understand about all female behaviorism. A woman acts in an unconscious way based on her own sex anxiety. The celebration of what is ugly among feminists is a celebration of liberation from their greatest fear. They celebrate the fruitless sterilization of all things and project that homosexual worship into all forms of their material displays. The fat, the queer aesthetic, the alternative ugliness of hipster goofiness are all mating displays of a dying animal. There is either submission to the male gaze or a rebellion to it. When beauty is celebrated in a civilization, it is because life is being celebrated. Queer aesthetic that coincides with fat acceptance is a celebration of sterilization and is a death cult. Once a man understands the deep morbid reality of feminist fashion and art, he will see it as a siren song into oblivion. Think about it like this. What happens when a young woman experiences sexual trauma during youth? She either will obsessively work to please the male gaze or she will obsessively war against it. This is the type who either becomes a stripper or who becomes a fat political radical. The fat one is using fat as a barrier of ugliness to the male gaze that has traumatized her. She eats as not just a comfort to her sex anxiety but also eats as a way to hide herself from the predatory gaze of men. Her fat exterior is a wall that keeps her invisible to the scanning eyes of threatening men. The fat itself not only makes her undesirable to men but also increases her infertility to protect her from the high reproductive anxiety. This is what a man must realize even about his own sexual desires.

Men desire a female who holds both youth and a slender form because both of these represent fertility. All male attraction is based on fertility just as female attraction is based on a male's virility or in the easing of her reproductive anxiety as in the case of seeking male provider-ship. Remember, all power is either transferred by fraud or force. When feminists spend tremendous amounts of energy on "fat acceptance", they are trying to gaslight men into accepting less from them.

The modern male is more sexually impoverished than any other generation. He either is sexless or gets a woman who refuses to bear any sexual burden for him. There is a high correlation between fat women and women who are dominant over men. The majority of women who act as dominant over their men are also overweight. The more power women get over men, the more they will shrug all further submissions to the rules of a man's game. Female liberation into careerism was an escape from the monogamous impregnations of inferior males and the increase in fatness among females is a further liberation from that primordial fear.

Hiding among innocents

The more power someone wants over others, the more they will be held accountable when things do not work out. To be in charge requires great mental fortitude and emotional detachment. There is a tremendous burden of stress to those who lead great crowds of people. The reason is that the people under their frame are dependent on them and this means that those who depend will place all blame on the leader when they fail. This is true of a president, CEO and it is true of a father. When shit hits the fan, it is the leader who everyone turns to. People readily give their first fruits to kings and leaders. but when the time comes for salvation, they expect the leader to pay back with solution. And if things do not work out, this is when the people rise up against the leader. The amount of stress it takes to be a leader is due to the responsibility over the lives of others. A father must not just worry about himself, but also, he must protect/provider for those under his authority. He must sacrifice himself for them and bear the burden of constant worry for their care.

To lead is to take on further responsibility in an abundance mindset. It means to seek out stress and responsibility. It means to expand responsibility from self out to a few, or a hundred, or thousands. The weight of a crown weighs heavy upon the head of a king. And what the king knows about all else is the freedom of will that he holds within himself. He is not one of the unthinking masses who depend on a head to lead them. His will transcends himself and stretches out over all. To lack free will is bear no burden of responsibility for action. It is a surrender of consciousness from the higher form of individual to the low form of the collective mob. To reason is to carry will of decision and it is decision that allows us to rule not just over self but others. Indecision is a state of passivity that robs the self of free will by option paralysis. This is the fundamental reason why females lean towards believing in the absence of free will while masculine men believe in free will. When someone lacks free will, they become blameless to their behaviorism. This is the comparison between man and animal and adult and infant. The reasoning mind that comes from a place of sanity in a well-formed human brain allows us the capacity for reason which informs our decision-making ability. Or surrender of consciousness for passivity of decision. This is based on lack of free that submerges the mind in the currents of others control.

The female in our sexual selection is designed for submission and is designed to surrender her power to the male. She floats and glides through sexual selection whereas the male must swim upstream against the currents. He must make choices over his behaviorism to overcome himself by humbly submitting to the burden of performance placed on him by females. The increased level of adaptive behavior allows him the higher consciousness of not only seeing the repeating patterns of his own failures but also the repeating patterns of success. To see patterns is to exist above what we examine. It is to see the madness of the stagnation of ourselves and the world that surrounds us. Method grows from madness. To repeat the same thing over and over expecting different results is insanity. To recognize a reconfiguration based on the previous patterns is sanity. This is what free will means. It means we can overcome the animal impulse that leads us into repetitive behaviorism. We can flip the script. We can experiment and we can deny the impulses that lead us to traps. We can bear the responsibility of all things which means we can absorb all blame without being overwhelmed by it.

In our times, we see a rise of men and women who hide among toys as a way to display an infantilized blamelessness. They wish to return to a state where they held no responsibility and where no one expected them to bear the burden of the world. This is why we see a massive increase in the identification of mental illness as way to shrug responsibility. Women and weak men know that we expect less from the mad and so they begin to surrender to madness as a form of escape from a world of responsibility. They wish away free will because it means that they must summon that will. They wish away free will because it means that they cannot be blamed for their own behaviorism. Sanity most times becomes a choice of strength over the void of madness. The greater the madness, the less we are burdened with sanity. When a man chooses sanity, he chooses the responsibility that comes with it. Remember, a female exists in the moment with no thought for future planning because she is designed to be myopic in closeness to nest where she nurtures her young. She lacks the capacity for wide lens understanding of not only herself but the world that surrounds her. The high anxiety that she feels from her indecisive nature makes her rely on the decisions of others. This makes her a submissive compliment to the will of her male who acts a protector/provider, but it also means she readily gives power away to the world that surrounds her. A woman seeks to hold the world but resents it as soon as it is in her hands. She holds it like a forbidden fruit that turns bitter in her mouth from the expectations of decision making that goes against her nature.

Since women are collectivist by nature from offsetting the burden of existence for when they are incapacitated with child as well as using their peers to regulate the hormone flux irrationality they feel, they will innately blend into the crowd as a way to appear blameless with them. The more any human blends in with fellow humans, the more he will surrender his free will and will no longer have to carry the weight of his individual existence. This is why feminists seek to equalize power, they want to equally distribute responsibility so as way to become blameless in decision. We are either born perfect or we are born corrupt. Knowing corruption is the start of changing self to overcome that imperfect nature. Whereas to be born perfect is to blame our corruption of self to the outside world. We can either see the innate impulse as moral or immoral. When we view what is natural to our impulses as moral, whatever suppresses that impulse becomes immoral. The Rousseauian view is to view the self as a liberated animal from inception that seeks to be free in a world that tries to control its natural state. It is being versus becoming. To be returned to the perfected state in surrender to ourselves to what is natural from within and to reject the outside conditioning that seeks to control that impulse. But what Rosseau and the feminine frame view overlooks is that to be responsive to our state of nature is to be in conflict with it. And it makes sense that Rosseau's philosophy led the French into democratic ideals which was an equalized distribution of power from a figurehead to the faceless masses. Not just a sharing of power but also a sharing of blame.

We see a rise of those who teach "born this way" in our times which is a hidden message to celebrate the animal within and to abandon free will. When we celebrate the animal and abandon free will, we blend ourselves in a state of blameless conformity to the surrounding HERd. The surrender of free will is a return to the low consciousness of animalism (caught in loops.) Women are symbolically headless creatures that rely on each other in blind feeling to navigate their realities. They are inherently arm in arm in a collective sisterhood to ease themselves of the anxiety of individual thought. The more power they seek in the world, the more they want to equalize the responsibility for the power they gained over others and the authority they gained over themselves.

We see a rise in gender madness in our times with a victimized celebration of mental illness because the asylum's padded walls bring more comfort to this generation than the open air of dignified sanity. They lock themselves away with digital castrations and hide among toys as way to trigger pity in the predators seeking to devour them. They hide among innocents like soldiers taking refuge behind children. They infantilize themselves in roleplay with childhood fantasy as a way to hide from the world. This generation indulge their every impulse as pure and holy. The future is for the sane while the mad only have the moment. The less they believe in free will, the less guilt they will feel in letting primitive impulse lead them. This mad generation do not need any more sympathy to their state of cowardice. They need to feel the consequences of a world that they have abandoned. Our generation will be marked not just about helping the mentally ill but also in revealing the massive fraud of those who hide themselves in insanity as a way to free themselves of the burden of life.

A world built for the weak

Women soften environments to increase comfort. A reason why women will have "pillow obsessions" where they collect pillows on sofas and beds. Why? They are nesters who have need emotional comfort which means they indulge in making their nests "homey" and relaxing. But also, they use comfort as a way to not only ease their own anxiety but also to create dependency in others. This is why a mother will try to serve her husband and children as a way to build not only an attachment for herself (women increase attachment by serving) but also to create a need for comfort by her. Women want to feel needed and this means they will create environments where feminine comfort is most depended upon. They will position themselves as emotional comfort to failed attempts and cheerleaders to valiant efforts as a way to not just fill a need *but to create a need*. The more a man allows himself to be emotionally comforted by a woman, the more he will begin to rely on her for emotional comfort. Soon, he will build a deep attachment in her acting as a mother figure who is there to ease his anxieties. Emotional comfort is the drug and she becomes the dealer. But what a man must realize is that a mother/son dynamic is a transfer of power from male to female which dispels the woman of her own sexual arousal. The more that a man depends on a female, the less the female will be attracted to him. Emotional comfort from women is a devil's bargain that lures men into weakness which ultimately destroys the relationship. Remember, a female is designed to nurture offspring in the nest while her man braves the outside world to provide/protect. This means that a woman's algorithm of nurturing her young to create a bond for dependency is her strategy to increase her power not only in the nest but in the entire world. The rise of participation trophy culture, helicopter parenting, sensitivity training and coddling of the young has created a softened world that is dependent on the comfort of the mother archetype. Modern females use nurture and emotional dependency as a *means for power*. Power is either gained by fraud or force. The more that this generation are emotionally protected, the more they will be sensitized to emotional controls.

The main methods of feminine control are through guilt and shame tactics based on a system of confession. A female who places herself in a position to be the ready ear to listen to a man's challenges and the shoulder that a man can cry upon secures herself as an emotional figure of authority over the man. She is luring him into the web of emotional dependency. Once he is trapped in the sticky fear of internal anxiety, he will become passive like prey to her desire for control. Females weaken their prey through emotion (or sexual desperation) as way to rule over them. Mothers increase the feminine frame of authority in the world by creating emotional weak confessor sons. They groom their children into surrendering authority to them which makes these men surrender to women in romance. This surrender of power to mother to girlfriend to wife spreads out to males being conditioned to viewing females as natural born leaders over them. Mothers will encourage their sons to "open up" as a way to know the truth of their power source and to create an emotional dependency. The same can be said of women in romance. Women will encourage their men to open up emotionally as a way to not only moralize emotion as the rule to obey but also to make men build a need for confession. This is all a method of transfer of power based on fraud. Why fraud? Because emotion is only as meaningful as we want to perceive it. There are two worldviews. The rational and the emotional. The less rational a man becomes, the more emotional he will be. We can only exist in one worldview at a time. When men are lured into the emotional worldview by women, they are entering a game of female design where women hold the rulebook. When a female turns her desire for power to the world, she will view the world as a nest and will soften the world in order to gain supremacy over it. She will sensitize people to the effects of emotional control. This is why political correctness and emotional protection of others' identities are being obsessively pushed by feminists. They are making people sensitive to language as a way to increase language control. Pretty smart huh? Remember, females must rely on their wits as the physically weaker member of our sex. It can be broken down in the following.

Encourage males to be open and expressive. This weakens individual fortitude and builds reliance on external figures for emotional regulation. The more need for emotional regulation, the more males moralize the importance of emotion. Once emotion is moralized from dependency on its regulation, the males become sensitive to emotional shaming. This is where language becomes an effective tool for power transfer. When a man has become feminized by relying on others for emotional regulation, he will be dependent on them for peace of mind. He becomes anxious when isolated from groupthink and holds a deep fear over excommunication from the group. This has primed him for the effectiveness of social shaming. Women will then use shame labels as ways to control those who have been weakened into reliance on group dynamic. The use of shame labels is a way to alienate the male from the emotional dependency that he has grown accustomed to. He will lose sense of himself when he no longer feels validated by those he has emotionally relied upon. This loss of self is in truth a loss of sense of belonging in the frame of authority of others. A child will feel this way when they let down their parents and a female will feel this way when her masculine leader disapproves of her. Alienation of belonging is a void of uncertainty in the frame of authority of another. The more we depend on others to regulate our emotional state, the more we create a sense of belonging to their authority for approval. Approval over what? Our sense of self. This is the trick of fraud that females use to gain control over males. *A female feels most loved when she feels most needed.* She will use love as a way to create a need for her. But the tragedy of this entire plan is that a woman is cold in her own expectations of her sexual partner in our selection. A female has a steep burden of performance that she places on males in sex regardless of how soft she wants the world to be.

Women have encouraged participation trophy culture in our generation to protect the emotions of boys so as to weaken them for emotional control and to make them easily defeated. All of this is done unconsciously to transfer power from males to females. The hardest thing for a man in our time to realize is that all women unconsciously or consciously work towards a female supremacy. Each of the sexes in our species are designed to challenge each other for control. This conflict creates strength and that strength is what has allowed our species to become supreme in adaptation to a hostile world that seeks to destroy us all. The major issue with the emotionally driven comfort of effort over effectiveness is that it confuses males in our selection to the cold brutality of female expectations for them. Women will push a participation trophy culture in the world while at the same time dismissing a man's failed efforts. It is not about the effort, it is about the result. This is true of any leader who holds responsibility over others. A president, CEO or father must provide results as those under their authority will not be satisfied with mere effort alone if it does not get positive results. This is the lie of the mother/son dynamic in romance.

Women lure men into emotional dependency as a means for power but will never give the men the unconditional love of a true mother/son relationship. They will emotionally comfort a male who is weak and needs support over a failed effort but inside their minds they will be coldly judging the male because they are programmed to depend on his results in the world. A reason why women seek out bad boys in sex is that the fundamental reason a boy is "bad" is because he places results above preapproved effort. He gets what he wants regardless of the morality of what he seeks. The "nice guy" on the other hand does not get what he wants but makes valiant efforts in his attempts. See? His woman hands him a participation trophy while handing herself over to the bad boy as the real prize. This generation will soon wake up to the siren song that has entranced them in a daydream. They will wake up to the falsehood of emotional meaning. They will wake up to how women weaken them for control. Then they will realize the game they were tricked into playing.

The rise of madness and the fall of mankind

All human psychology is influenced by sex anxiety. The expression of our human reality is compelled by our collective sex anxiety as a species. Feminine is chaos because feminine is infinite subjectivity that creates a vacuum to meaning. When something is everything, it becomes nothing. The innate duality in a female creates a spirit of uncertainty that increases anxious neuroticism. A woman uses her social interactions as a way to regulate her deep uncertainty over her internal reality. Female subjectivity tests males' objectivity. The role of a female in our species is to test the confidence of the male in our selection as a way to reassure herself of his authority. But more specifically, a woman tests a male's certainty of self as a way to lower her reproductive anxieties. Women will fall into unconscious gaslighting of others as a way to test the confidence of current power systems. If a woman's illogic weakens the confidence in a man's logic then it means the male's authority in selection loses trust. A woman expresses herself as a way of seeking a check to her own reality. When a female goes unchecked by a male, her anxiety rises and she becomes emboldened over him. She will lose trust in his frame of authority which makes her protect herself from bearing children in that state of anxiety. Females only desire to bear children when the male authority above them reassures their high reproductive anxiety.

When a man frames a woman with his certainty of self, what he is doing is *calming her reproductive anxiety which creates sexual arousal*. Remember, a woman's sexual arousal is based on her feeling safe to let go of her reproductive defenses. Fear of loss of control is the singular issue with female sex dysfunction. When a woman cannot trust male authority, she will be highly guarded to the submission which will most arouse her for the sex act. She guards her sexual arousal because her reproductive anxiety is high. What a man finds out the longer he carries strong masculine frame around a female is that the female will align herself with his identity, and his confidence is a massive reassurance to her anxieties. She wants a brave leader who cannot be easily controlled by her emotional manipulation and who passes her testing with calm rational certainty. But what happens when a female is able to emotional control a man and the man becomes reactive to her testing? She will lose confidence in his authority and will guard her sex from him while seeking out other males to calm her sex anxiety. A female needs a man to calm her anxiety and she will close her sex to a man who spikes her anxiety while opening herself up to men who calms her anxiety. Now let us open up this psychology from what is small to what is large.

All psychology has biological meaning and all grand meanings must be anchored with small understandings. How a female acts with a male in a sexual relationship is how all females act with males in our world. What do we see in our modern world where record number of females are living single or are dominant over males in relationships? What do we see with the massive increase of fatherless women who lack respect and trust for male authority? We see ideologies arise that support depopulation while borders being opened to foreign males. Do you see it yet? The more women are unframed from dominate males in their local communities, the more they will guard their sex from them and will open up sexual diversity to other males who cannot be easily controlled by them. This is a major reason why Europe which has been ruled by females for decades has dissolved their borders to Muslim men who have a male dominant culture while at the same time having collapsing birth rates. Females must seek out dominant males in our selection to calm their reproductive anxieties. When men wake up to the fact that women open borders for sexual reasons and that they cling tightly to world ending climate hysterics that moralizes reproductive death from their own reproductive anxiety, this generation will realize the animalistic and selfish reasons that undermine female leadership.

The more power that women get over males in their civilization, the less they will respect their civilization and seek to be conquered by others. This is why feminists are working overtime to destroy the national heritage of the nation that gave them power. A house ruled by a female holds an emasculated male who is mocked openly and whose children despises him. This is true of a family dynamic and this is true of a nation. Once women get power over men, they will emasculate and cuck them. When feminists rise in power inside a nation, they will undermine its power and give it away to outside nations just as a disloyal wife gives herself away to other men in a corrupted family. She will teach the children to undermine her husband's authority, she will teach the children to disrespect the father as she opens herself up sexually to outsiders. This is female behavior from family to the world itself.

When men transfer power to their women's hands, their women will transfer that power into the hands of strangers. A woman is inherently in tremendous self-doubt and when a nation falls into its feminine frame of authority, it will begin to doubt its own power and will readily give it away to others. We see a rise in mental illness in western civilization because the rampant subjectivity of a woman's perception of reality is collapsing meaning by the breakdowns in definitions over the most fundamental of structures. Sexual confusion creates a snowball effect in madness because our psychology is anchored by the certainties of our biological imperatives. When children are made confused about simple biological imperatives, they will become confused in all things. A generation who does not believe in objective truth will be made subject to lies.

Feminists are psychologically castrating children because they are spreading their own reproductive fears. This is why feminists spread homosexual propaganda to the youth in nations. This is why women are pushing gender fluidity on children in our times. They are pushing their innate uncertainty of self on them and moralizing lifestyles that lead to depopulation. The breakdown of objective definitions to reality is a symptom of hyper feminization. Madness can only be solved by gaining method. It is in the narrowing of our vision that we are able to see the world that surrounds us. We must focus on singular truths to stabilize our minds from being unmoored from reality. The disciplined and narrow focus of masculine consciousness eases the unfocused confusion of feminine consciousness. Anxiety occurs when we neglect solving a problem or when we feel helpless in solving a problem. When we give method to madness, we are able to rise above the anxiety of chaos. When we prepare children with the most basic truths of their reality, we give them the disciplined focus needed to navigate that reality. Confusion causes anxiety. This is the reason why women hold innate anxiety from their subjective psychology from genitalia blindness as well as the irrational feelings from hormone flux. A woman is looking for a confident male in sexual selection because his confidence solves her confusion. *What makes a good leader is how we perceive reality*. Young women can playfully deconstruct reality with social constructionism and take delight in an undefined perception of reality but they are only spreading confusion and chaos. They are not leading others from anxiety but rather leading them into anxiety. The element that makes a good leader is one who calms their followers' anxiety. And how is that done? A leader must be certain in his objective rule over reality to earn trust from his followers. This is true with a male in sexual selection who wins over a female by being certain and confident. This is true of a CEO leading a corporation and this is true of a king over a kingdom. The breakdown of objective meaning is a symptom of feminine frame authority but also it is a grooming into servitude. Females fall into submission to males because they readily give away their power to the certainty of self that males hold over them. Women spreading sexual confusion to children in our times is conditioning this generation into submissive doubt of self that will lead to mass subjugation of will to those who hold self-belief over them. The softening of this generation into emotional sensitivity and gender fluidity is making them clay in the hands of power figures.

Sacrificing the young

Each generation is a temporary wave that rolls to shore. Each generation must hand off the reins of power to the next. The generation who was born first must give the next generation the tools for survival. But one of the most challenging psychologies that a man must face is that those who profess to have our best interests in heart will be the ones who most cripple us into dependencies. The devouring mother archetype is the female who weakens her children so that their dependency on her grows and cripples them. This is a major reason why the young of the past few generations have been coddled and weakened for submission.

Women have gotten too much power over the minds of their children because the fathers are either weak or missing. We have either devouring mothers who cripple their children to prevent them from leaving the nest or we have weak men who enjoy the feeling of an easily won authority over the weak. When men become weakened, they become desperate and that desperation influences them into a beggarly view of reality. When a boy is raised in a mixed litter with brothers with different fathers or when he is raised by a step-father, there will be high sex anxiety as all the males will fall into competition with each other. An environment where the males have high sex anxiety with each other means they will be guarded over their own power in desperation. They will confuse the next generation as a way to embolden themselves over them. They will try to impress their own fears and anxiety onto the next generation as a way to cripple them into easy submission. This dark psychology is expressed even among the nicest human beings. All creatures on earth fear the transfer of power from themselves to others. A man will clearly understand this dark psychology when he begins to change himself from the affection seeking boy to the respect seeking man. Other men will see him as a threat to the power they hold and will persecute him. Women will begin to test him more as they reassure their reproductive fears with the newfound change in his character. This animal fear will present itself when a man begins to seek power.

All power on earth is in constant flux from one generation to the next and from one set of hands to the other. When a man gains power, another man loses power. This is the cold reality of our existence upon this rock. A devouring mother will create a high dependency in her children as a way to protect her power over them. Their independence is a sign that her power is fading and she fears the emptiness of her nest. She fears being left alone and forgotten. She fears letting go of the control that eases her anxiety. A castrating father is a man who keeps hidden the means of his masculine frame and allows the mother to dominate his sons. He rules from a tower as he looks down on the suffering of his sons like an irresponsible king over his kingdom. We have a large crowd on this earth who make weak so that they may feel strong. The transfer of power from father to son is one of the most sacred acts of belief in mankind. It is a shout of belief to the next generation.

We can dig even deeper into the dark psychology of sacrifice of the young. There is a twisted enjoyment in the hearts of the elders of a village who celebrate the foolishness of the youth only because it makes them feel better about their early mistakes. A lot of the old among humankind watch from afar as the next generation stumble without offering help because the stumbles make them feel stable. This is why an old childless female will feel threatened by a young couple who settle down with a family. The couple will be a warped mirror to her own regrets and insecurities. And so, she will applaud the youth who follow in her twisted steps and jeer the ones who forsake her path. It is desperate way of preserving ego. Those who fear complexity are most times the ones who moralize simplicity. Our generation were not only abandoned by our fathers but we are also crippled by the sex anxieties of the world we were abandoned into.

All human consciousness is based on the struggle of power which in itself is based on sex anxiety. This is the core that all human psychology is built upon. When a man is fatherless, he will be most astute to the sex anxiety that surrounds him. A reason why orphaned men become Machiavelli in their understanding of what it means to survive. They begin to see the curtain torn that reveals the hidden truth to the act of niceties that people present. They will see that those who are most loving to them will also try to confine them with their own fears. There are two prisons that every man must escape from. He must escape from the imprisonment of his own fears and he must escape from the imprisonment of the fears of others. The greatest fear in a human heart is the transfer of power from our hands to others. To lose control is to surrender authority. A man must be aware of the mental prisons that others try to contain him inside. They are trying to confine him as a way to castrate his power. They are trying to confine him as a way to sacrifice him for their own gain. They attempt to make him small as a way to feel large. What this generation must awaken to is that they were born without a guardian and were left among wolves. Our fatherlessness has spiked sex anxiety among our nations. Our fatherlessness has made this world desperate and corrupt. Those who hold the power will not give it up easily. All power is ether transferred by fraud or by force. And this is why this generation are being gaslit into a weakened state. Those in power do not want to transfer power because it reminds them that their wave is rolling to shore. Generational power change means that a generation is soon coming to an end. Do not let the fears in the last generation cripple you into submission. Rise up and lift the orphan next to you. This world will soon be ours whether we are prepared for it or not.

The heat of power

Females will always war against male power because females will always hold reproductive anxiety with weak males. There are dominant females who believe more in their own authority than the males in their lives and so they expand the current authority to the world that surrounds them. This was true a thousand years ago and this will be true a thousand years from now. The rise of fatherlessness has created a void in the consciousness of modern women's minds over male authority. They have never had to respect men from childhood and see no reason to respect them in adulthood. Men have failed them. Their fathers abandoned them and chased their sexual heat like mindless animals. The men in their lives have begun to imitate egg carrying nesters which projects insanity. Women have good reason to distrust male authority in our times. *And a female always has a good reason to distrust male authority since her reproductive design is based on it*. It is up to men to calm females under their frame of authority. It is in a female's design to not only distrust male authority but to submit to masculine authority.

Females are not acting on their own accord, they are reacting to the state of men in their environments. All female empowerment is an animal reaction to male disempowerment. A woman is designed to test male authority and to assume command when she is with a male who spikes her reproductive anxiety. She then will look for other stronger males as a way to protect herself, her children and any future children she might bear in sexual selection. She looks for power among men as a way to calm her deepest sex fears. She looks for a man who can frame her as a way to calm the chaos of her animal. All women want to be under a man's authority but they must be inspired into submission. A woman craves to give her power away in a relationship from the primordial fear of knowing she will be incapacitated with child in womb. This unconscious fear informs all her behaviorism in a relationship. Once a man realizes how the burden of pregnancy affects a woman's psychology in sexual selection, his eyes will be opened to the truth of sex.

There is no psychological meaning without biological necessity. Let us explore the sexual heat between a male and female in the sex act. The more confident the male is in his authority and direction during the act, the more aroused he becomes. But this also simultaneously arouses the female who wants to be directed and led through the act. The greatest transfer of power happens in the bedroom. A man may notice that some of the most bad-tempered women will be submissive with their men and will obey their authority. Why? Because they sexually benefit from that arrangement. They pursue the pleasure principle. They become sexually aroused by submission. All human behaviorism is based on some aspect of selfish pursuit. Women would never submit to men in relationships unless they got sexual heat from it. A woman is designed to transfer power in sex because she it is a biological necessity to rely on a male as leader while she is incapacitated with child in womb.

This is where the male must not only protect and provide, he must lead too. Let us ask why, why, why to this point and this will open up the rationale behind it. Why do women say they want bold, assertive, confident and take-charge men in sexual selection? They want to be led but do not want to say it. Why? Because most males do not inspire submission. This is why women reward men who take the lead on dates. Why? Because it signals that the men will take the lead during the sex act. Why would this be important? Because the leader/follower dynamic calms a woman's reproductive anxiety that she holds over the unconscious realization of not only the burden of pregnancy but also the reality that she will be incapacitated from that burden.

A female is innately aware that she must not only transform her body with tremendous biological resource but also surrender her vision of the surrounding world so as to become hyper focused upon her offspring in the nest. She knows that she requires a male who can brave the outside world and who can handle the major concerns that surround the nest. And this very innate wisdom informs all of a females' sexual pleasures. She craves to surrender her authority and power in sexual selection because she is wise to the reality that lies ahead for her. Let us zoom into the actual arousal that occurs in the sex act. A man who exaggerates his authority in sex will not only arouse himself but will arouse the female as well. This act of heightened power transfer is a ritual to the future power transfer that happens when the female is weighed down with child and must nest. Good sex is a premonition to the survival of the species. But also, the taboo plays into heat because the reaction to the rules of conflict allows both sides to become inflamed in a special rebellion. We see feminists proudly marching for power in the streets but will readily submit to male authority in the bedroom to achieve sexual pleasure. But this is only when the female wants sexual pleasure.

A good portion of feminists sacrifice their bedrooms for the throne. They compartmentalize their sexual enjoyment of submission as an animal secret in their lives. They are oblivious to the meaning behind the sex act because the sensitivity of their emotional worldview keeps them from the coldness of dispelling illusions upon illusion. To be rational is to ask why upon why upon why until the truth narrows in a bare and cold reality. We must unpeel not just the meaning but also unpeel the warm comfort of illusion when we want to understand truth and this is why the majority embrace lies. And this is why women are easily controlled by shallow emotional reasonings that allow them necessary lies. They are meant to be myopic in focus because they are meant to be nurturers in nest. The genitalia blindness allows them the subjective insecurity to feel through their environments and the hormone flux inspires their collectivism which allows them to survive hand in hand within that darkness.

When a man shows that he can take the woman's hand and lead her in sexual selection, it acts as a massive relief to her psychic darkness of self. She readily gives him authority and begins to align herself with him because it means not only her survival but also her sexual pleasure. That aroused heat is what encourages her survival. She knows that for her to survive with her offspring in next, she must trust giving authority to the male. When a male shows no sex anxiety in sex and takes the dominant lead, he allows the female to surrender her control of all the guards and barriers over her reproductive system. She lets go of her tightly gripped control and transfers absolute power over to the male. This allows her not only the grandest of sexual heat but allows her to let go of authority to the male in sex which is symbolic meaning of her letting go of authority to the male when she is confined to the nest. Her willing acceptance of the male's authority in sex is a roleplay to the trust of surrendering to his authority over the nest itself. The sexual heat that most arouses both male and female is a preparation for the burden that sex bears.

Going with the flow

A woman may feel that she is getting wiser but in fact her psychology is altering only because her biology is changing. The age of a female has more to do with her wisdom towards her biology than the experiences she has accumulated. It is the biological imperative of reproduction that influences her early partying years with high fertility to her more serious time of settling down when she innately feels that her eggs are half gone. Then once she has just a few eggs left in her forties, she will then want to party as a way to feel alive before her biology calls it quits. This is a common pattern among females not because they have learned lessons in life but rather their animal is leading them forward. It is a man who must discern his behaviorism based on the accumulated efforts of his actions. This is how a male succeeds in sexual selection through a mountain of rejections and how he succeeds in life. He must rationalize his life while a female goes with the flow of her biology necessities. A female acts reckless with her sexuality at a young age not so much from inexperience as much from an arrogance to her abundance of youth. She feels alive and wants to experience excitement because she is at max capacity for child bearing and is compelled by that heat.

The attention that a female most craves from her anxious self-doubt from a young age is finally abundant along with her fertility as sexual attention becomes easy. Her want for sexual attention and the reason she gets sexual heat are both paired up with the exact same biological reason. She is most fertile which means she most wants to seek attention while her showy display of youthful fertility gets her attention from surrounding males. She is not only drawing the male gaze to herself with her fertility display but also stealing the gaze from other women which creates the indignation that most pleases a woman's want for drama. A young woman does not want to nest because she wants to be seen by the world and wants to experience its excitement. She does not want to nest because she has abundance of options from her peak fertility and that peak fertility makes her want to present herself to the male gaze. This is why young women desire to go out on the town and be seen. They want to go to clubs and parties because the female sexual strategy is to present the self for validation to the male gaze and see if there are possible opportunities for being engaged by desirable males. Women like to go out and be seen because it is part of their sexual strategy the same as when men like to go out and look for women.

All girls' nights out that are in public are ways of catching the male gaze to validate their display of fertility and to be playful with sexual opportunities. What a man must realize is that a woman will never admit that this is true. It is an unconscious behaviorism and women can easily lie to themselves over the animal behavior that motivates them. They will say that they "just want to have fun" or just get out of the home but in truth they just want the excitement of sexual display, flirtations with mating and want to leave the nest to achieve that. A woman is led unconsciously by her biological necessities in sexual selection and she gives meaning to her behaviors after the fact. Remember, a female is in the dark about herself and is blind to the truth of her reality. She feels through her life and environment. Then she must narrate the experience to herself after she experiences it. Women do not want to feel that they do not have free will or that they are being led unconsciously through life. Who does? Females will emotionally refuse to accept that they do not hold agency over their lives because it hurts not only their ego but also frightens them to the loss of agency in sex that spikes reproductive anxiety. They also do not want to view themselves as more animalistic than males.

From a young age, a female is shocked into body horror with the mysterious blood flow and chaos of emotions that pull at her each cycle. It is as if the sun and moon play games on her body as it ebbs and flows in monthly cycle. She is most afraid of her animal which makes her flee from facing it. Each time she can view males as more vulgar and animalistic is a deep reassurance to her fear of self-reflection. The most eager pointer to fault in another is trying to distract themselves from their own imperfections. A female becomes a woman whether she wants to or not while a male must choose to become a man. Ancient elders in tribes across the world had rituals of manhood for young boys because the act of becoming a man had to come from a conscious understanding of suffering and how they survive that suffering. They would traumatize the boy out of a man. The boy had to become a man. Females grow into their womanhood. It is a state of unconscious being and not an act of conscious becoming. Life just happens to a woman while a man must shape himself to life.

Life for women is like passengers on a train that are moving across country. Their movement on the train matters very little to the overall journey that they exist on. The train moves them forward at great speed regardless if they sit or move about. Each passenger on a train will have different personal experience about the vehicle that carries them. A woman's body is the train that carries her regardless of her personal experience of the ride. Each woman will think themselves special in the small movements that differ them from the other passengers on the train. But they all end up in the same locations as each other but in small variance on the sexual selection that carries them forward. This is why it is relatively easy to decipher a woman's ambitions in life because they are based on the repeatable patterns of their base design. A woman's behavior is based on her current egg availability. The more eggs she has, the more she will be playful in sexual selection because she is not made serious by the time constraint of her diminishing supply. Once she is made serious by her limited time then she will seek further commitments in males and will be ready to nest. And then once she is even more limited in egg availability, she will circle back to the playfulness of her youth as a way to take risks with her remaining fertility. Lastly, once she is totally depleted of fertility, she will find more psychological meaning in being in the nest because there will be less biological meaning for her to make sexual displays like before. During each biological phase a woman's experiences, she will give it reasoning to make her feel more in control of her life and not controlled by her life. Just as a woman's body exists in a phase through the month, her life in sexual selection exists in phases based on her fertility.

A man's body is more stabilized in hormone and his fertility is more stabilized which makes any change in his course based not on biological necessity but conscious decisioning. A man's only phase is in the transition from boyhood to manhood which is not due to the simplicity of biology but rather the psychological destruction of his boyhood mental framework. The tribes of the past had to rationalize ways to shatter the feminine frame of authority in the minds of the males in their tribes and they utilized trauma itself as way to usher the boy into a new phase of manhood. A woman's fertility controls the phases that shape her life decisions throughout her life. While a man must force himself into a new phase of life, a woman goes with the flow of her own phases. Her passivity in the surrender to her biological necessities is a reflection of the passivity she has in her own sexual selection. A woman presents herself and decides whether or not to surrender to experience.

Tempted by the fruit of another

Sexual infidelity between our species is based on reproductive opportunism. What we call "hedonistic urge" is our base greed in pursuing reproductive access. This is true of males and this is true of females. But the reasons for the base urge is just as different between the sexes as their biological necessities are different. A male falls into sexual heat when he is around a female who projects the obvious clue to fertility and heath. When a male cheats on his female, he is unconsciously trying to seed other females as a way to continue his genetic legacy. The mindless animal in a man is to spread his seed as far as he can before he dies. He transfers a fear of death to the sex act itself. He fears being forgotten and falling into oblivion. His animal heat compels him into what seems like irrational lust but that has the most rational biological imperatives.

The promiscuous male is a male who holds sex anxiety because he holds death anxiety. Men do not want to die forgotten and so they attempt their best at being remembered. A lot of males want to haunt a female by impressing their sex on them and infecting their emotionalism. This is a way to be remembered and a way to have a sense of belonging. They are trying to capture eternity through the most primordial means. No act of sex can be simplified to just an act of lust and no sex act is meaningless to our anxieties. A man's hedonism is a desperate attempt at securing indulgence while he can. "While he can" is an unconscious motivation based on death anxiety. This is why to be hedonist it to place the pleasures of the day without regard to the consequences of tomorrow. The impulse to seek out pleasure that could cause chaos in our lives is a way to become a ritualistic display of only believing in the moment.

When we place the impulsive urge of our body ahead of future meaning, the fear of death grows in our minds. We only can calm death anxiety by acts that forsake the moment for a belief in the future. This means we act as those we believe in the future which makes us less afraid of seeing it. The more indulgent and impulsive a man acts in regards to his animal pleasures, the more he is conditioning himself to fear the future. And that fear that grows based on his own behaviorism is what gives shape to all his future events. The man who attempts to sleep around with as many women as he can is like a man who is eating as fast as he can because he fears that it will be his last meal. It is deep fear of death that creates promiscuity in males and that death follows them.

Why does a female commit sexual infidelity? A woman seeks a male who can calm her reproductive anxieties. She is not like the seed spreading male but rather focuses on securing the most valuable male that can provide her the best seed and nesting experience.

"But Jerr" a voice calls out from off the pages, "Nesting experience? What about the females who seek out the fun guys who party?"

Think about what a fun party type guy is truly giving a female. A woman likes a fun guy because his carefree fun personality projects that he does not fear death and this reassures the female that he believes enough in life to calm her reproductive anxieties. Women look for men who can ease their reproductive anxieties and that can mean "carefree fun guy" and that can mean the "serious provider" and that can mean the "tough guy protector." Each individual female will seek out different males who specifically solve their own personal sex anxieties. How the female got a specific sex anxiety can be due to her upbringing or her ancestral memory. For example, if a woman was raised poor and she experienced her mother being in sexual heat to other males besides her father because their nest was suffering then she will be more apt to look for provider males. Or for example, if a woman's ancestors experienced traumatic events where the fathers were killed before the women, this could be held in the collective unconscious or influenced the mothers placing a value on protection in sexual selection through behavioral conditioning. The key thing for a man to realize when his woman wonders off with another guy is that the other guy was solving a specific reproductive anxiety that the woman held. If she left a guy for someone with more money, it is because she was solving her nesting problem. If she ran off with a "fun guy", she was looking for a guy who could project confidence in his carefree view of reality. To be a man is to bear the responsibility of all things. This means that a man must take responsibility for not solving his female's reproductive anxiety. Why? Because a female is not designed to calm her own reproductive anxiety, she is designed to seek out a male who calms that for her. Her aroused sexual state is a precursor to calmed reproductive anxiety and her burden of performance that she places on males in our selection is all based on her sex anxieties. A reason why "incels" get zero sympathy in our times is because a male's success in sexual selection is his own responsibility and must be earned. A woman does not view sex as charity because there is too much biologically on the line for her. The sex act is vulnerable to her because the surrender of her body in pregnancy is vulnerable to her. She must trust the male to ease that greatest anxiety in her body and once that anxiety is relieved, she is able to let go enough to achieve pleasure. Her sexual pleasure is all based on the relief of her reproductive anxiety. And a woman's infidelity itself is based on her reproductive anxiety. While a man's infidelity is based on death anxiety, a woman's infidelity is based on life anxiety.

A male seeks out sex because he fears death and that fear compels him to propagate himself before he dies.

A female fears life and so she looks for males who have become desensitized to their death fear and who can calm her life anxiety.

Males are compelled by death fear into sexual selection and that death fear fades from their behaviorism from the desensitization of failed attempts and frequent rejections. When a man can disconnect from his failures while refusing to give up on future attempts is a powerful display of belief not only in self but life itself. If a man gave up lifting weights because it was hard, he would not grow muscle just as a man who gave up from failure in business would never achieve wealth just as a fun guy who gave up on his carefree demeanor because of social embarrassment would no longer be fun. The core of what makes a male calm a woman's life anxiety is that the male does not give up in living his life when he encounters failure. This is the core of a man's sexual selection in becoming better and adapting himself to new environments. The growth of self is a symbolic gesture to women of growth of life.

A man will never be able to control the variables of a woman's reproductive anxiety but he can mitigate the anxiety by fulfilling the basics. A man who makes money, grows muscles and displays low anxiety in social situations will project that he is not afraid of the world that surrounds him. Men should take infidelity personally but not let them drag them down. There was deep truth in the reasons why a woman strays and the deepest truth is that the man failed in calming the woman's reproductive anxiety in some way.

Females are more herd minded and followers by design than males which means that their social circle will have a major effect on their behaviorism. They will fall into mindless imitations to female family members or friends who normalize cheating on males. They will fall into this behavior and genuinely feel lost about what happened. The reason is that they are used to aligning their behaviors with the herd and when the herd commit sexual infidelities, they will just follow along. This is why a man should be conscious of a woman's peer group and her family. A lot of disloyal females come from disloyal families.

A woman wants to look up to a man

Women tend to be more sexual drawn to men who are five to ten years older than them. The reason is the dominance that is established during youth. A male who is ten years old will hold not only physical dominance but higher intelligence of a male who is five years old. Dominance is commonly established among children with brutal violence. This creates a sexual hierarchy between the old larger males and the smaller younger males. Women look to the victors of social situations and it commonly is the older males who win early social dominance situations during youth. This conditioning carries with a female from her own childhood into adulthood. A male is in constant growth over his masculinity and manhood from teens to twenties to thirties to forties which also influences the female's view of older men. The more established the male, the more the female will feel safe to nest with him. But also, the closer in age a fertile female is with a male the greater the chance the male has virality to his own high testosterone and therefore sexuality to preproduce. This is why a female desires a male who is older than her but not too much older. Five to ten years tends to be the average spike in arousal to the majority of females.

But what a man needs to realize is that females are more suggestible to a power hierarchy of male design. For example, women will be more sexually drawn to an older male not just because he is more mature in age but because his physical and mental maturity holds power over younger males. It is more common for boys who are a few years younger than their elders to be more apt in falling into submission to them. A male who is a few years younger will hold some reverence for his older peers. This is conditioning based on the truth of physical and mental dominance that is established in social situations between males of mixed age groups. When a boy is able to easily able to physically dominate his younger brother, this mental frame will carry into the future regardless if the boys equalize in physical strength. The same for a father who impresses his physical superiority over his children at a young age will be seen as superior even when the boys outgrow him. This is true of a father over son, older brother over younger brother and this is true of a trainer of a lion who nurses a cub from infancy to monstrous size.

The mental frame is set when there is vast difference between physical power even if that changes later on. A female will not usually be physically dominated by older males like a boy is dominated by the older ones in his own sexual group. But a female will respect the frame of experience and wisdom of a boy who is a few years older than her. Women do not just independently judge the objects of their desire but rather look first to how others interact with their sexual interests. For example, a female will observe how an older boy is revered by younger boys and she will align herself with that frame of thought. Females innately look for a leader in sexual selection and when a man can lead others, it becomes a sign of his sexual value. The female looks to the younger boys who surrender their power to the older boys which creates sexual value for the older group. Then the females sexualize the older boys based on that power transfer. All of this conditioning begins in youth but continues with a woman for the rest of her life. She will always view males who are a few years older as more dominant in her mind because that is her conditioned memory of it. Young boys will readily give up their power to older boys in elder reverence. This continues among men from infancy, to teen years and into a man's twenties. Usually when most men enter their thirties, they learn to not readily give away power to older males but rather compete with them as equals. But this does not matter to females who will still view older males as sexually more desirable based on the frame of thought from childhood. She will remember the times that boys her own age readily gave away their power to older boys and how the younger boys had to physically look up to the boys a few years older. And how the younger boys were physically dominated in social situations. All of this will be hard grained in the minds of females.

Head over heart

For thousands of years, males have been designated as the head of their household in family arrangements. The major organized religions have designated the father and husband as head over his wife and family. This ancient wisdom has stabilized not just the family unit but all civilization. The male is biologically conditioned to be objective with his singular focus on his genitalia, he is not reliant on others to the same degree as women for his emotional regulation, his hormone is more balanced which gives him greater certainty of self, and the humility of his need for adaptation in sexual selection creates a more powerful understanding of past failure for future success. The cold judgment of a male's masculine frame clears away the clouds of emotional reasoning. Remember, emotion clouds judgment. We all have varying degrees of emotion and rationality. The more emotion, the less rationality just as the more rationality the less emotion. Only two worldviews, the emotional worldview, and the rational worldview. The male is biologically designed for less emotion which makes him less dependent on external judgment of others for his sense of self.

The less a man relies on others for his sense of self, the more authority he gives himself outside their control. Not only does a man attain a greater sense of self when he has solitude but he is able to separate himself from the collective in order to view himself as above them in authority. Also, the collective has respect for distant authority just as familiarity breeds contempt when others begin to easily identify themselves as peer. Why must all this be said in regards to males as heads over females according to religious tradition? Because males are better equipped for the coldness that good leadership requires. All things exist in polarity and that polarity must be balanced in scales. The distant-cold-leader behaviorism of a male allows his female to fall into her feminine frame of close-warm-nurturer. When a female feels safe to nurture in nest, she is safe to be myopic to the needs of the nest. She does not need to worry about the past and future. The burdens of ancients and the hopes for tomorrow can be surrendered to the male who exists outside the close confines of the nest. He is able to stand above them all and plot a course as leader for them all. This allows the female to exist in the necessary moment for child rearing. She feels safe to exist in the darkness of the nest just as she feels safe to exist in the darkness of her feminine consciousness just as the child feels safe in the darkness of her womb. The male's frame is the guiding force that protects/provides and leads them all.

A man will notice that the majority of traditionalists are male just as the majority of futurists are male. This is because males are biological symbols of past and future. They have one foot placed in history and the other placed into the future. What this means is that their level of rationality makes them able to see horizon to horizon in planning capacity. Just as the head on a body is able to look backwards and forwards with eyes scanning an environment, the same for male consciousness in our species. The female is short sighted to historical meaning and ill equipped for future planning. This is why females fall into collective bargaining for their welfare and fall into indulgent behaviorism at the expense of future gain. They are designed to live in the moment as nurturers which means that they suffer without males to plan their futures for them. That is why in fatherless times, there will be impulsive indulgence in the pleasures of the day while very few sacrifice that indulgence for future provisioning. When a female leads a family, there is less disciplined structure and more of a spirit of acceptance where tolerance is the leading principle. There is either emotionally driven punishment where a parent shows weakness in losing their temper when they discipline or there is a total absence of discipine. Sometimes there is mix of the two which only confuses the children into not trusting the authority of the parent. Females are not meant to be the disciplinarian in family structures because emotion corrupts the execution of that discipline. When a male is weak or absent in a family, the female will act in authority as disciplinarian in her own emotional worldview. The child will either be abused or neglected by the inconsistent structure. This spins the child into chaos which creates high anxiety from lack of trust in the authority above. That anxiety will morph and take shape with anti-social behavior that either is expressed in anger towards self or others.

A child needs direction, guidance and discipline. A child craves the rational discipline of a caring father. It holds meaning in principle, never expressed in impatient anger and is consistent in execution. The child's anxiety is relieved by knowing what to expect from his father's sense of order. What makes a good disciplinarian in a family is the same as what makes a good judge of the law or leader of any sort in the world. Impartial coldness towards the execution of judgement is what creates a sense of justice. The act is one based on principle and not bias.

"But Jerr," a voice calls out from off the page, "Some men can be more emotional than women"

Yes, this is true. There are two kinds of human biology just as there are two psychologies. A male can be in his feminine frame and a female can be carrying the masculine frame. Men can be culturally conditioned into a feminine frame when they are coddled into it. When a mother teaches her son that sharing himself will ease his suffering, what she is doing is building a dependency on her authority and moralizing emotion to the boy. He will then begin to use his peer groups as emotional regulators just as women do when they battle their hormone flux and need reassurance to their feelings of irrationality. But a male does not have the hormone flux or the genitalia blindness that creates anxiety over certainty of self. Those two aspects of female biology compel them to give authority to others as a way to calm their innate anxiety. When a male learns to not moralize emotion, when he learns to not rely on others to regulate his emotional state, when he learns to keep secrets and not feel that he must confess to relieve anxiety, he will optimally align his male biology with his masculine psychology.

The male is meant to be the leader and head over females in our world because females are not designed for leadership. They are designed to be submissive to authority and they are designed to nurture in the nest. A female's arrogance in her passive entitlement in sexual selection makes her lack the adaptation of humility necessary for good leadership. Women want to be the boss but they do not want to know what it takes to be the boss. They merely want to be and not become. They have not respect for tradition and history just as they have no need to learn from failures in sexual selection. They are the choosers which means they do not need to figure out sexual selection like a male. The male must become an appreciator of history just as he must appreciate all his failures in selection. He must have self-belief enough to keep trying among failure while keeping track of small adaptations for future success. See? This is the fundamental reason why males are historians and futurists. This is the reason why a male is the head who carries the past into the future. He is order to a female's chaos of the darkness of the moment. Remember, to have no memory of the past is to hold great uncertainty over the future. Every attempt we make without learning from the past keeps us in an eternal loop of madness. Women do not need to struggle through countless rejections in sexual selection which makes them oblivious to the means of how *hindsight produces foresight*. The head must lead the heart otherwise we let our feelings rule our lives. The head must lead the heart because the heart must comfort the weak. Males must lead their households with masculine frame because this allows the females to focus themselves on the offspring. When this happens, the female does not have to worry about the future so that she can make herself present for nurturing. She does not have to use her emotionalism for discipline but rather can use it for comforting in nest.

A woman waits

A woman presents and waits in sexual selection. This means she is dependent on the will and actions of others. This influences her neurotic thinking and causes her to take less responsibility for herself in the world. The lead of initiation and approach is the fundamental reason why women want men to lead. They need the man to break the social anxiety and to *risk rejection* by being *bold in their assertiveness.* Being made a fool is a most feminine fear. The risk of putting the self out for social judgment is a cause of feminine passivity. A woman has more a fear of rejection because she is emotionally connected to her sense of self in her selection. A sense of self that she was born with and merely needs to present for approval. If a woman is sexually rejected, she will take it personally but will not have a way to solve that anxious feeling because her design is passive in presentation.

When a woman is made to doubt her sexual worth with a rejection, she cannot solve that anxiety with positive action but rather solves it with positive thinking. She does not need to adapt herself to a new environment but rather needs to gaslight herself as a way to preserve her static sense of being. She is complete and fully formed. She was born with her worth and simply had to grow into her body as a sexual strategy. When that presentation is rejected, she is trapped in herself with a feeling of helplessness. If simply being is not good enough then how can a woman feel confident? Women view rejection of their sexual worth as not just a learning experience like a male but as a tragedy that cuts to the core of their identity. This is why we have gaslighting campaigns making females feel good about themselves regardless of their body types and this is why women rarely approach males in sexual selection. The fear of rejection keeps them in passive anxiety to the will of others. This is the key psychology of why women seek out men who have leadership skills because it means that the males will risk rejection by taking the lead in initiation.

There is safety in passivity but also there is dependency. The ancient archetype of a princess being saved by prince charming is fundamentally based on the passivity of a woman in our selection. She wants to be spared the risks of rejection. She wants an attractive man to swoop down and save her from the passivity of her presentation. She wants a man to ride with symbolic action and boldness to assertive his sense of self before her. A man who can break the spell of her paralysis and who can awaken the sleeping beauty. Men hold libido and sexual drive but a woman's sexuality must be awakened. Remember, a female is an egg carrying nester who does not assert herself on men but rather waits for a man to inspire her to let down her defenses. She wants a man to melt away her self-consciousness with his confidence. She wants a man to boldly showcase his authority and lead her into his frame of reality. She desires a man with a strong sense of so that she can dissolve herself into that greater self. A woman does not want to risk rejection because failure would reveal the weak sense of self that she clings to. She would spin in self-doubt and that doubt would overwhelm her. On the other side, a male in sexual selection detaches his self-worth from failed sexual attempts and rejections. He is like a salesman who gets door after door slammed in his face but finally makes a sale. He has learned to detach his sense of worth from the failure of rejection because he alters himself finely for each future attempt. It is his positive action in adaptation that frees him from the neurotic anxiety of passivity. His identity is based on becoming and is never truly formed completely. A woman is born complete and all rejection is a deflation of that state. The male starts at the bottom and must slowly build his sense of self and accumulate his worth. He starts with high rejection and must overcome that whereas the female starts with low rejection from her youthful beauty which makes her sensitive to a sullied ego from sexual rejection. But also, a female relies on social interactions to regulate her emotional state which makes her sensitive to the judgment of others. This means that a woman's social anxiety makes her avoid the risk of bold assertiveness she seeks in a male in our selection. Making her intent known with sexual initiations is taking a chance on judgment and women fear social judgment most of all. Women submit themselves to each other with elaborate social shaming rituals which makes them social cowards. A major reason why women are attracted to disagreeable men who are politically incorrect is that these men represent a social freedom that they wish they could share.

Power

and

sex

A man seeks power to gain sex and a woman gives her sex to secure attachment with powerful men. This is the eternal animal rhythm of our species that influences all politics, economics and civilizational institutions on our world. All humans are either controlled by fraud or by force. We can either force ourselves on others or we can seduce them. The core rationale behind my philosophy is to inspire submission in women and not to force submission. A woman is designed for submission to a man's masculine frame. We learn power dynamics as men from our own sexual selection. This is why a man who reads books on leadership will have better success with women than by reading books on game. Sex and power cannot be separated by meaning in our species. *Females look for powerful men and men look for power.* It is the chase of our sexes. And if a man is not looking for power, he might be scooped up by a female who is settling with him by holding authority in their relationship. All human interactions are based on a transfer of power.

When men are made to believe by women that a sexual relationship is not based on power is a supreme state of foolishness. The man becomes like a child in his naivety. The female encourages him to surrender his power as a "enlightened man" so that she can ease her reproductive anxiety by controlling him. But the dark psychology of this arrangement is that the man is unconsciously aware of that transfer of power. This is the same with a weak son and his dominant mother who have the Oedipus complex. It is the whisper of shouldering the burden of power that weighs so heaver on the carrier. People give up power because all power comes with responsibility. The man who believes in an "equal relationship" is a man who does not want to shoulder the burden of absolute authority. He wants equality of not just power but also of responsibility and accountability for authority.

A man willingly chooses his own emasculation and infantilization. He aches for the golden memories of the carefree times of the mother/son dynamic. The times where he lost himself in childish play while his mother was the frame of authority that stood as a barrier between the home and the outside world. She acted as the calmer of his anxiety which allowed him the blissful ignorance needed to fall into daydream. It is the longing for anxiety free fantasy that acts as a siren song to many men's senses of power. They readily surrender power and its abundance of real-world wealth so that they can hide among toys as an innocent to the chaos that surrounds them. It is mass cowardice that exists inside these men as they turn away from a world that expects them to rule it. They would rather live in the poverty of digital fantasy and irresponsible daydreams then have to shoulder the responsibility for leading themselves and others. Men willingly surrender their power with conscious understanding of that surrender but will hide themselves in ego defensive postures of "true enlightenment" as a way to save face. With the rise of female power in our times, we will without a doubt see not just men romanticizing their emasculated state but also an increased attack on men who are not emasculated like them. These men who stay at home washing dishes and their women's laundry will not only profess to be truly empowered but will persecute masculine men as continuing evil acts of oppression. This is like a slave who enjoys being provided for by the master but mocks and persecutes slaves who escape the plantations. The liberated slave is a mirror that the cowardly slave cannot look upon without seeing his own weakness. And so, he seeks to shatter the image of the freed slave as selfish and demonic. But in reality, the attack on the liberated one is an act of self-hatred. Those who infantilize themselves will demonize those who seek responsibility.

There is not place on earth where power does not exist. There is no place on earth where mankind's sexual selection does not influence. Just as a creature's psychology must be formed from its biology, all human creation must be formed from human biological imperatives. If a man is not actively seeking power, he is actively surrendering it. We either rise or fall. We either get weaker or we get stronger. Women can only rise in power when men willingly give it up. And women do not have the physical strength to force their will on others and so they rely on fraud. They encourage males into emotionalism from a young age and use that sensitivity to emotional manipulate as a way to gain control over them. We live in an age where emotion is viewed as the higher morality only because it is the main method for the feminine frame of authority to gain power. It is as simple as that. Women gain power when men are emotional and so they will moralize emotion in culture as bait to trap males into submission. Emotions are just as meaningful as we want them to be. They are like drugs. A man can have an "experience" on a drug but the experience can only have as much meaning as his sober mind can give it after the fact. The same for emotions. They can only truly have as much meaning as we are willing to give them. We see crying men in movies and tv shows because women gain power through the emotionalism of men. Only when men see through the spells of emotional entrapment will men rise in power. Once men see that there is only power and sex. These two things are the greatest truths of our times. Emotion is only meaningful when it is used to ensnare others by its charm. It is a tool to be used and feared. This generation whom behold power everywhere will harden into cold warriors in the upcoming new world.

Desperate lies

A woman is innately dependent on a male leader in sexual selection which makes her lack empathy for the male's burden of performance. She does not feel shame or guilt in using a male in her selection and using fraud to deceive the male into that selection. All power is transferred by fraud or force. This means that a woman must rely on her wits to navigate sexual selection to her benefit. She uses emotional gaslighting and use of language to transfer power from a male to her. When a woman gets a male to open himself up in vulnerability, she is unpacking the truth of his authority to reassure her reproductive anxiety but also gaining information to use for her advantage against the male in power transfer.

A woman does not feel as guilty as a male in deception because of her feeling of helplessness. It is her passivity in our selection and her irrational feeling from her hormone flux along with her innate knowing of the extreme biological burden of pregnancy that allows her the freedom from guilt/shame in her use of fraud in our sexual selection. This desperate and confused state of female nature allows women to be survival-focused at all costs. And this state helps them to be flaky in temperament which allows them to take to flight to safeguard themselves from pregnancy when threat arises, or when pregnant, to preserve their offspring in womb in flight. A woman's helpless desperation makes her feel little guilt in pursuing desperate measures. The passivity that makes a woman neurotic in her circular worries is what compels her to look for a man to solve her problems. The burden of performance that a female places on a man is list of solutions to the need of her reproductive anxieties. *Females are problem having creatures who look for problem solving males.* This is the sexual appeal of the handy man and why confidence is most arousing to females in sexual selection. Confidence is display of potential competence. Male competence over themselves and their environments is the crucial elements to solve a woman's fear of life. Men who are confident project that they do not fear death which is a celebration of life. That celebration of life projects that they have low sex anxiety which calms a woman's own sex anxiety. What a man needs to realize about women is that they feel very little empathy for the male experience because they are dependents on that experience. This is why women in our times demonize and mock sexless male they call "incels." They do not show compassion to these men but rather see them as both a burden on society and a danger to the community. But this hatred is a part of the animal in a woman's design. It is not a woman's biological role to teach a man sexual selection, it is her role to look for a man to overcome himself and the world. The only way women can protect themselves from physically threatening males is by subterfuge and deception.

Women cannot force their will on the world by physical force, only by acts of fraud. If women were expected to teach men sexual selection, they would have zero defense against protecting themselves against inferior males. And also, a woman desires a male to lead her in sex and to direct a male how to act in sex is to dominate him. She does not want to teach a man the truth of her behaviorism because that teacher's role destroys not only her one defense in sex but also places her as puppet master to her biological needs. A lot of feminists in our times falsely think they can direct their own sexual pleasures by teaching males how to please them. They are fools who do not understand their own sex. But most times they are willfully ignorant of this fact because to admit it is to admit that their own submission brings them pleasure.

Since a woman's main tactic for protecting herself in sex is by deception and her man tactic for power over men is by fraud, this creates a culture of lying among females. Whether it is a woman lying to protect her sexual value with men or a woman lying to protect her friend's feelings, lying is a part of female nature. Lying is an act of desperation and females are most desperate in our selection. Women are used to lying to each other and hiding the truth of their language. All passive aggressions and ironic meanings come from a place of anxiety over a threat of physical violence. Hidden speech and subtle communications are ways to "outsmart the brutes." All of this is part of womankind's culture. They are passive aggressive in nature because of their weaker psychical state compared to males. Hiding in the shadows is a desperate act. But there is power in shadows as it builds mystery which can confuse and mystify opponents. This is the power of a female. She hides what can hurt her socially and in sexual selection, and she hides what can hurt the feelings of others. She is a natural born liar who seeks power by pretending that she is above power dynamics. There is not one second of a day that a woman does not think about power because power is the solution to her reproductive anxiety. She is power mad and uses fraud to gain power because she is anxiously seeking a solution to her reproductive anxiety. Women feel no sympathy with the male experience because of the female role to carry child in womb and the dependency that creates.

Think about it like this.

A female knows she must look for a male leader in sexual selection who can protect/provide for her while she is incapacitated with child in womb. But the problem is that she is surrounded by inferior males who do not deserve to reproduce. What does she do? She hides her true desires and gives advice tailored to the inferior males who surround her. This is why women give “nice guy” advice to men. A male who knows female nature and understands to look through her deceptions will ultimately most calm her reproductive anxiety which will most sexually arouse her for propagation. This is why women go for the bad boys who cannot be fooled by them. They are highly aroused because these bad boys do not let themselves be controlled by the inherent fraud that women use to control men and each other. A bad boy is someone who is street smart which means that he is not naive to the truth of the struggle of power. He knows it is a dog-eat-dog world and that even so-called good people lie to each other. He does not believe words but rather only pays attention to how people act. Men who came from rough upbringings have seen the worst of human behavior and have been lied to their whole life. They do not take things at face value because they have experienced lies being sold with a straight face. When a woman is around a bad boy, she wants to have sex because he can look though her act. He sees the real her which makes her feel seen for the first time in her life. The nice guy who agrees with everything she says is clueless to the real her. She does not love the nice guy because he is in love with a lie. She can love the bad boy because it feels real to her. The bad boy can see through the mask that has kept her safe from judgment her whole life. He can look past her desperate acts to control him and see through her lies. She is exposed before him which makes her feel vulnerable and that vulnerability makes her feel naked. A nakedness of true intimacy in knowing a person in truth. He knows she lies not because she is a bad person which makes her feel good about herself. He accepts her as a desperate fraud who must protect herself from judgment. She is like a child and he becomes like a knowing father to her. The nice guy in his pleasing nature is viewed as a child to her and she becomes his mother who not only hides the truth from him but easily deceives his naïve state. When a man understands that women lie by nature to protect themselves socially and to protect others emotionally, he will not see them as immoral but as desperate in their human condition.

The birds, the bees, and the human species

A man who understands a woman understands himself. We are different roles of the same kind. All living creatures base their behavior on staying alive and replicating that life. They can war against it, become victim to it, or accept it. The behavior of human males is based on harmony or disharmony with human females. The state of womankind is based on sex anxiety and whether or not mankind is solving that primordial need. All of a woman's perception of reality will be shaped by her primordial sex anxiety whether she realizes it or not. Women are like flowers and trees that move only because sun and winds form and shake them. They are unconscious to the primal force that moves them just as the birds and bees are unconscious of the base compulsion that keeps them rooted to their existence. It is not a matter of consciousness as much as a compulsion from unconsciousness. A woman will act a certain way based on her reproductive anxiety regardless whether or not she knows it. She is moved by the currents that exist inside and outside her just like all living creatures whether big or small.

Do we say that a bird or a bee is wrong for acting a certain way or do we try to understand why they act the way they do based on their own primordial needs? This is the same frame of thought a human male should have for a human female. The female is imprisoned by sex anxiety and her entire worldview will either be influenced by how a man calms that anxiety or incites it.

If a bird or a bee was acting out of harmony with design, would we ask ourselves the reason for it? Why would we blame women for their sex anxiety when that sex anxiety is a product of our own failures? A man is meant to understand a woman without her telling him how to understand her. He is supposed to "just get it." This means that a man must become condescending to the needs of those under his gaze. He must observe and behold the ripples upon the surface of the waters he steps into and walks through. The watery surface becomes a reaction and reflection of his association with it. This is the same with female nature. A man should view the nature of women as ripples and reflections of himself and other men. The behavior of a woman is more predictable than men think because she is rooted to the sexual compulsion to mate and replicate. Women cannot escape the force that shapes them into life and replication of life.

The feminist woman is "pro-abortion," fearful of overpopulation and spreads homosexual propaganda to children in order to sexually confuse them so that they do not reproduce as a means of warring against her own high reproductive anxiety. She wars not just against her own womb but the womb of all women. She moralizes childlessness as a means to justify her own reproductive fear. This is what the simple creature does in response how men fail to calm her sex anxiety. Does that sound like a moral sage that guides the future based on hope and wisdom? Or does it seem like a simple living creature is merely expressing its own sexual frustration in a selection that inspires her primal fears?

The truth of mankind is that a man gains something by remaining ignorant of female nature and ignoring these simple facts of the opposite sex. What is that? He believes in the false vision of women so that he can close his own eyes. He moralizes them as "complex moral sages," so that he can place the burden of his own existence upon their shoulders. Women will become "mysterious" in a feminist time period only because men need them to be so that they can throw all their hope, shame and responsibility into the darkness of their imaginations. The female who is complex and mysterious to men allows them to fall into daydream. It is a siren song and a siren song can only work when sailors fail to turn away from the lull of surrender. When men view women as "complex and mysterious," what they are doing is protecting themselves from the truth of their simplicity. Truth is a burden to those who protect the bliss of their ignorance. But they can only sleep for so long on a sinking ship before the water touches them and then it will be too late.

Once a man shrugs his ignorance for enlightenment, he is presented with the burdens of truth. The curtain is torn asunder and can no longer hide the mystery that imprisons the imagination. Truth is a burden and a man who does not fear truth grows strong in carrying the expectations that truth requires from him. He can no longer hide behind the mystery of women because they lay exposed to the reality of the truth that exists within him. The truth of women is that they are simple creatures and that simplicity has clear meaning to what truth means to men who are paired with them in our species. What happens when authority breaks down in a nation or city? Those who were previously held back by the authority will often use the chaos as a fog to hide themselves as they indulge their own anarchic greed. Chaos is a cloak to those who want to feast upon fear. The man who beholds women for the first time by interpreting all their behavior on reproductive anxiety will see them for the first time. No longer can he hide among the chaos of confusion. No longer can he throw his power into the darkness of female authority that holds so called unknowable intent. No longer does he shield his own eyes with ignorance to the truth that calls him to answer. He sees women just as he sees the birds and bees. A common logic based on the means of survival and replication. He does not mourn his own newfound cold understanding of reality but rather learns to accept it before embracing it completely. Once he sees the truth, his eyes will be forever opened and he will no longer be able to hide in the comfort of lies.

Made in the USA
Las Vegas, NV
24 December 2024